GOD WITH US TODAY

Devotions for Families

June Galle Krehbiel

Faith & Life Resources
A division of Mennonite Publishing Network
Mennonite Church USA and
Mennonite Church Canada

Library of Congress Cataloging-in-Publication Data
Krehbiel, June Galle, 1949-
God with us today : devotions for families / by June Galle Krehbiel.
p. cm.
Includes index.
ISBN 0-8361-9343-1 (pbk. : alk. paper)
1. Family—Religious life. 2. Family—Prayer-books and devotions—English. I. Title.
BV255.K74 2006
249—dc22

God with Us Today: Devotions for Families

International Standard Book Number: 0-8361-9343-1
Design by Merrill Miller
Cover photo: Photosearch
Printed in the USA

To order this book or request information, call 1-800-245-7894.
www.mph.org

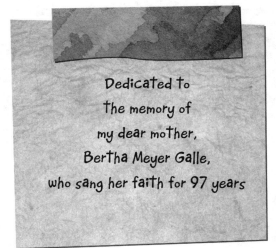

Dedicated to
the memory of
my dear mother,
Bertha Meyer Galle,
who sang her faith for 97 years

Phil, Karen, Craig, Dana, Brant
Wishing for each of you the
Love, Joy and Peace of Christmas, 2006!
With love,
Mother and Dad
Grandma and Grandpa

Contents

Introduction

I cuddled into Mom's lap, my legs barely reaching the edge of the cozy rocker. She read story after story from our ABC Bible picture book as I looked at the drawings, heard the faith stories, and learned my ABCs.

My favorites? B for baby Jesus, C for children, T for Timothy. I'm sure that God was there with us then and at other times when our family shared devotions together.

When is God with your family? It's easy to say that God is with us all the time. But how can families live more consciously in God's presence?

One way is to cultivate a regular worship time in the home. Today's pace of life can easily squeeze out quiet moments of reflection and prayer. But families who make devotions part of their routines reap many benefits.

When we gather to worship, we hear stories and assurances of God's work in us. We encourage each other in the midst of the challenges we face both at home and in the world. We are reminded that Jesus' call in our lives sometimes goes against the values and life-patterns we see around us but also that God's Spirit is here to help us—all the time!

Written for families with children, *God with Us Today* offers resources for 100 Bible-based devotional times. Each devotion is centered on a Bible passage and a meditation—to be read aloud. Side elements help families reflect on what they hear. These include a Bible verse, written prayer, visuals, and thoughtful questions. Many of the devotions also offer a poem, song, game, or quotation.

As you meet together with your family, may you feel the presence of God with you. May God bless you with love, joy, and peace that you can share with others each day.

—June Galle Krehbiel

EMMANUEL TODAY

One of the key names that the Bible gives to Jesus is "Emmanuel"—which means "God with us" (see Matthew 1:23). The fact that God has chosen to enter personally into our world is at the core of God's "good news." Jesus came to live among us, revealing God. And through the Holy Spirit God continues to move with us and in us throughout our lives. Daily worship times are a good way to keep us aware of God's constant presence.

A note on sources

This book includes a number of sidebar quotations from various sources. Where these are copyrighted, they are marked with an asterisk, indicating that full information on the copyright holders is included in the source list on page 210. Most songs and hymns that I quote are found in four worship books used in my Mennonite tradition; these, too, are marked with an asterisk, and included in the source list.

Unless otherwise noted, Scripture quotations are from the New Revised Standard Version.

—J.G.K.

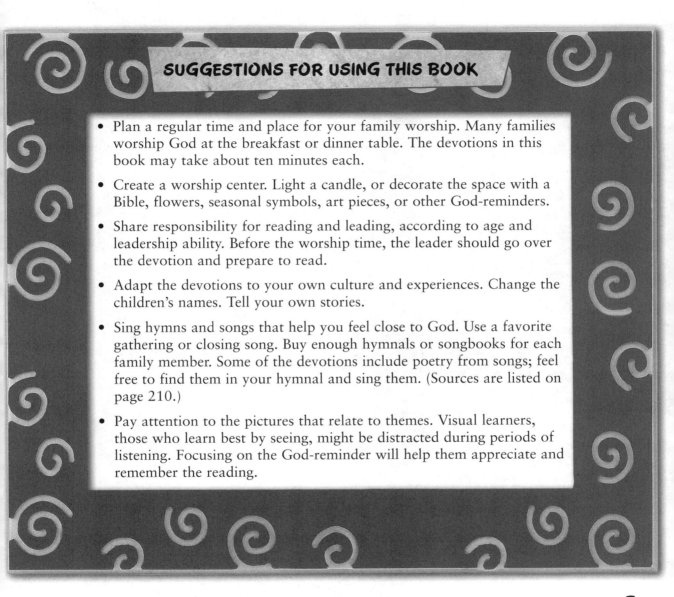

SUGGESTIONS FOR USING THIS BOOK

- Plan a regular time and place for your family worship. Many families worship God at the breakfast or dinner table. The devotions in this book may take about ten minutes each.
- Create a worship center. Light a candle, or decorate the space with a Bible, flowers, seasonal symbols, art pieces, or other God-reminders.
- Share responsibility for reading and leading, according to age and leadership ability. Before the worship time, the leader should go over the devotion and prepare to read.
- Adapt the devotions to your own culture and experiences. Change the children's names. Tell your own stories.
- Sing hymns and songs that help you feel close to God. Use a favorite gathering or closing song. Buy enough hymnals or songbooks for each family member. Some of the devotions include poetry from songs; feel free to find them in your hymnal and sing them. (Sources are listed on page 210.)
- Pay attention to the pictures that relate to themes. Visual learners, those who learn best by seeing, might be distracted during periods of listening. Focusing on the God-reminder will help them appreciate and remember the reading.

1

READ

Genesis 1:1–2, 20–23

You are worthy, our Lord and God, to receive glory and honor and power, for you created all things.—Revelation 4:11

Woodpecker Talk

"That woodpecker was talking to me today," Jenna announced at the dinner table. "First it went 'SQUAWK SQUAWK SQUAWK,' and then it tooted at me with its horn." Jenna tapped her fingernails on the table as she said, "Toot. Toot. Toot. Toot. Toot."

Her family laughed at her imitation of the red-headed bird she had seen in their backyard. Jenna loved birds and often told stories about them at mealtimes. Her family was used to her tales of wrens, owls, sparrows, blue jays, cardinals, and meadowlarks.

"How did God get ideas for making birds? There are so many of them, and they are so pretty. I love them all!" Jenna exclaimed.

The Bible begins with God's creation of the heavens and the earth and all living things. We can see and know who God is through creation. We know that God loves beauty and that God is creative. We also know that God must like many, many different things because each thing and each person God made is special in its own way.

As you worship today, sing the sound of your favorite bird or animal and remember that God designed all creation.

W oodpecker sounds

One woodpecker can tap 8,000 to 12,000 times a day.

What do you like about God's creation?

How does creation help you understand God?

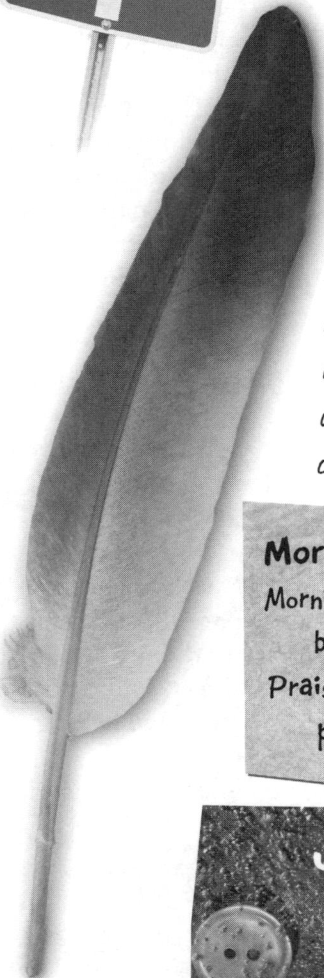

People sounds

One of the reasons woodpeckers tap is to talk to other woodpeckers. What sounds, other than talking, does your family use to communicate? Which sounds gather the family for a meal or get everyone out the door at the same time? Which ones don't you like?

LET US PRAY

Thank you, God, for all your creation—for birds and animals, skies and waters. We worship you today because you are the Creator of this great big wonderful world. Amen.

Morning Has Broken*

Morning has broken like the first morning;
blackbird has spoken like the first bird.
Praise for the singing, praise for the morning,
praise for them, springing fresh from the word.
—Eleanor Farjeon

Jenna • small bird • English

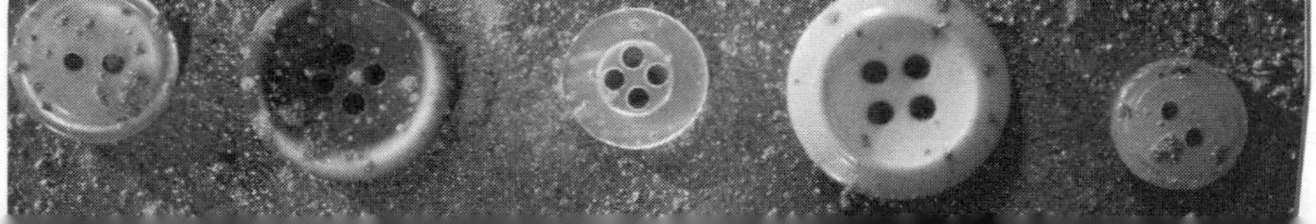

2

Bus stop

READ
Genesis 2:4-9

God created humankind in his image, in the image of God he created them; male and female he created them.
—Genesis 1:27

At the busy bus stop in the center of the city, Brody and his grandmother watched people come and go. They saw men and women, boys and girls. They saw big people and thin people, and many colors of skin.

Often when Brody and Gram waited for their bus, they had fun trying to find one person that Brody might look like when he was all grown up. They both knew he would never look exactly like anyone else, but they enjoyed playing the game to pass the time.

"So many, many people," Gram would say as Brody tried to find his look-alike adult. The rule was that before they got on the bus, Brody had to pick that one person.

"We're all brothers and sisters," Gram would say, "and we've all come from the earth, but God's ground is different colors in different places."

The creation story in Genesis 2 tells us that God created humans from the dust of the ground and gave them God's breath. We humans like the earth and feel close to it because we were made from it.

The Bible tells us that we were made in God's own image. We are not as great and powerful as God, but we are like God in other ways. We are like God when we create things, and when we share God's spirit of love, goodness, and caring. There are so many ways that we look like we belong to God!

Today we thank God for creating all people, beautiful in their own way.

Who are some of your favorite people?

How are you like God?

LET US PRAY

Thank you, O God of all creation, for making all people in your image. Wherever we go today, help us share your love and goodness with those we meet. You are a great God. Amen.

The Street Car*

I love to watch the street cars
That run along so fast,
And people at the windows smile
At me as they go past.

So many, many people
Get on and off each car;
I wonder where they're going
I wonder who they are.
—Minnie E. Hicks

Brody • brother, of the muddy place • Irish

3

READ
Genesis 11:1-9

I will boast only in the LORD.
—Psalm 34:2 (New Living Translation)

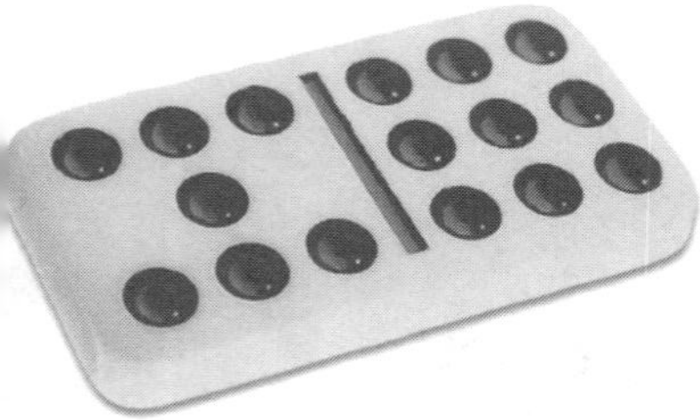

Important Dominoes

"Let's see if we can stack the dominoes all the way to the ceiling," Ernie announced to his family. "Can we pile all of them end-on-end without falling?"

"Why?" Ernie's dad asked.

"Just to see how great we are," Ernie replied, showing his muscles.

The family stacked the dominoes higher and higher. Then, CRASH! The dominoes tumbled to the table. Again, the family tried, barely breathing so they wouldn't disturb the stack. One, two, three, four. The tower of dominoes wiggled. Five, six, CRASH.

Like the builders of the Tower of Babel, we have problems when we do things to make ourselves seem really important. We brag. We boast. We boss others around. In doing so, we make life miserable.

Can we ever make ourselves as important as God? Of course not!

God wants us to think not about what is important to humans, but about what is important to God.

When was the last time you bragged about being important?

How are you important to God?

UP

Suppose I were glued to the ceiling all day,
Stuck up so high in an upside-down way,
Up on the ceiling and greater than all,
Higher than high and much taller than tall.
"Why's he up there?" my big sister would shriek.
"I don't think he wants to play hide-and-seek."

I thought I would like being up there so high,
Seeing the world like the sun in the sky,
Far from my bed and my games and the floor
Far from my dog and my toys and the door.
Then I'd be lonely up there all day long,
Learning that down is just where I belong.

—J.G.K.

LET US PRAY

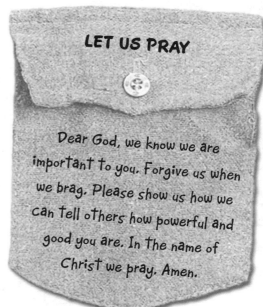

Dear God, we know we are important to you. Forgive us when we brag. Please show us how we can tell others how powerful and good you are. In the name of Christ we pray. Amen.

Ernie (Ernest) • truth • German

4

New Home

READ
Genesis 13:14-18

Abram moved his tent, and came and settled by the oaks of Mamre, which are at Hebron; and there he built an altar to the Lord.
—Genesis 13:18

Sonya and Addison sat quietly in the backseat of the car, still strapped in their seatbelts. Their dad was getting a key to the apartment where they would live. Sonya wondered if she would like their new home, their new neighbors, and their new town.

"Come on. Let's look at our new place," their mom said. Inside, Sonya and Addison looked at each room, finding where they would sleep and eat and play.

Their mom suggested that before they unload the car, they all gather together for a "new home" prayer. "Your mom and I can be the roof," said their dad, reaching up.

"And we'll be the walls," said Sonya, grabbing Addison's hands and stretching out their arms.

Then each one said a prayer, thanking God for their new place to live.

In the Bible, we read that Abram and Sarai moved to where God directed them. They remained faithful to God and remembered to worship.

Sometimes changes in our lives make it hard for us to think about God. It's especially hard when nothing seems to be the same as before. With God's help, we can remember to worship, even when we're getting used to new things.

What changes have happened in your life recently?

Who or what reminds you to worship God?

LET US PRAY

(Hold hands to form a "home.") Dear Lord of Abram and Sarai, we ask your blessing on the place we live today. Thank you for the way it keeps us safe and comfortable. Help us to always remember to worship and praise you—even when our lives change. Amen.

New home poem

We thank you, God, for this new home,
This place where you live too.
We'll worship you and share your peace
In all we say and do.

We thank you, God, for floor and roof,
for window, door, and wall,
For space to share with family,
A gathering for all.

—J.G.K.

Sonya • wisdom • Latin

Addison • Child of Adam • English

5

Doll Collection

READ
Genesis 18:1-8

Welcome one another . . . as Christ has welcomed you, for the glory of God.
—Romans 15:7

Julia was dusting her auntie's doll collection. "Where's this one from?" she asked.

"Sweden," her auntie said.

"And these?"

"Bosnia, Vietnam, and China," Auntie said, pointing to each one. "The dolls remind me of my friends from many places. This one from Japan I've named Sumi. Do you remember when Sumi lived with me last summer?"

Julia did remember her. She seemed like a stranger at first. But Sumi played games with Julia and read stories to her about Japan. When Sumi had left Auntie's home, Julia had missed her.

The word *hospitality* comes from a Greek word that means love to strangers. That's what we do when we invite travelers and other guests into our homes. We welcome the guests, give them food, let them rest, and show them love. Being nice to guests in our home is the first step to making friends for a lifetime.

In Genesis 18, we read the Bible's first story about welcoming strangers. While sitting at the entrance of his tent, Abraham looks up and sees three people standing near him. Abraham rushes to greet his guests. He offers them water so they can wash their dirty feet and freshen up. He invites them to rest under the tree. Then he offers them bread and cakes and other food. Only later does he realize that he has hosted God's angels.

When we have guests in our homes, strangers become friends. When we sit around the table with others from outside our family, we learn new things and feel closer to God. When we take time to welcome others into our homes, it's as if we are welcoming God's "doll collection" into our hearts.

You are like a tree, giving your shade to the outside.
—Arabic proverb

Why does God want us to welcome guests into our homes?

What could your family or church do to offer hospitality?

LET US PRAY.

O God, teach us what it means to offer love to travelers and other guests in our homes. Help us to be willing to give water, food, and rest to those in need. Amen.

Hello, world!

Did you know that more than 6 billion people live on our planet? They live in 191 countries and speak more than 6,000 languages. The language spoken by the most people is Chinese Mandarin (874 million people).

Learn all these ways to say HELLO, and you will be able to greet half of the people in the world. The languages are listed in order by the number of people who speak them.

Chinese Mandarin – Nî hâo
Hindi – Namasté
English – Hello
Spanish – Hola
Bengali – Ei Je
Portuguese – Olá, Oi
Russian – Zdravstvuite
Japanese – Konnichi wa
German – Guten Tag
Korean – Annyong Haseyo
French – Bonjour
Javanese – Selamat

Julia • youthful • Latin

Sumi • clear, refined • Japanese

6

READ
Genesis 37:2-4

God is a God not of disorder but of peace.
—1 Corinthians 14:33

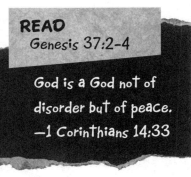

Signs of a strong family

What does it mean to be family? Pray for God's wisdom as you use this list to evaluate your own family. Which ones are easy? Which ones need work?

- Commitment
- Spending time together
- Appreciation
- Good communication patterns
- High degree of religious orientation
- Ability to deal with crises in a reasonable manner.*

Bicycle Shop

Tomi helped his father at the bicycle shop. Tomi liked to fix flat tires and put together the new bikes. He liked to wait on customers when they came to buy a new bike or get one repaired. Tomi's dad knew a lot about bikes, and Tomi learned from him.

One day Tomi heard a family come into the shop. Two brothers were arguing, their parents were arguing, and even their pet dog was yipping so much that it seemed to be arguing too. Each one wanted to be more important and talk louder than the others. Tomi wondered if his own family ever sounded like that.

Some families in the Bible, including Jacob's, didn't always get along. Jacob had his favorite child, Joseph, and this caused big problems. Joseph bragged to his brothers about one day being more important than they. The brothers were extremely jealous and unkind.

In the Bible a family was often called a house or household. This included all the people who lived together. God made households so that all people would be cared for and so that they would learn to live together. If we can live at peace with our family members, it is easier for us to get along with other people in our world.

When you hear the word *family*, what good things do you think about?

Are there times when it is good to argue?

LET US PRAY

O God of all families,
lead us as we live
together with our family.
Teach us to be kind and
patient and loving.
Amen.

BIBLE FAMILIES

Can you name these Bible relatives? For help, see the list below or use a Bible dictionary. Answers are on page 209.

1. The mother of Jesus
2. The father of James and John
3. The sister of Mary and Lazarus
4. The brother of Miriam and Aaron
5. The grandfather of Solomon
6. The great-grandson of Ruth and Boaz
7. The daughter-in-law of Naomi
8. The son of Eunice
9. The wife of Aquila
10. The husband of Elizabeth

David, Jesse, Martha, Mary, Moses, Priscilla, Ruth, Timothy, Zebedee, Zechariah

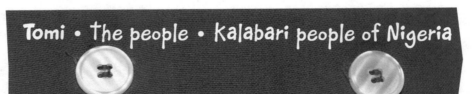

Tomi • The people • Kalabari people of Nigeria

7

READ
Genesis 50:15-21

You, O Lord, are good and forgiving, abounding in steadfast love to all who call on you.
—Psalm 86:5

Forgiveness is a gift of high value. Yet its cost is nothing.
—Betty Smith

Broken Lamp

Benjamin was mad. He had to stay home. It wasn't fair. He sat by his bed, kicking everything he could find—his toys, his boots, his bed. Then he kicked the table beside his bed, and CRASH, the lamp fell to the floor.

Suddenly he wasn't mad anymore; he was sad. Big, droopy tears filled his eyes and slid down his face.

His big sister came to the door. "What was that?" she asked, but Benjamin couldn't talk. She saw the broken lamp and the slivers of glass and ran to find Grandpa who was staying with them.

"What's wrong, Benjamin?" Grandpa asked, sitting on the bed and talking very softly. Benjamin didn't say anything, so Grandpa talked for him. "Benjamin, I think I know why you were mad. You wanted to go with the others. And your madness made the lamp break, and now you are sad and embarrassed. I'm guessing that you're also sorry for what happened."

Grandpa knew exactly how Benjamin felt! "I'm sorry for breaking the lamp," Benjamin said, crawling onto the bed to give Grandpa a hug. He liked feeling Grandpa hug him back.

In today's Bible story, Joseph forgave his brothers for treating him badly. He could have been mean to them, locked them in jail, and never talked to them again.

The brothers worried that Joseph would treat them as badly as they had treated him (Genesis 37). They cried and offered to be his servants. But instead, Joseph chose to forgive and to be kind.

When we do wrong, we like having someone around who is kind to us and helps us say, "I'm sorry." Saying those words and showing that we want to be forgiven can make us feel a lot better. They can help heal our broken love.

Why is it so hard to get along with everyone?

Fill in the blank: Saying "I'm sorry" makes me feel

______________________________.

Forgiving Words

Think of words that are good to use when you need to ask to be forgiven.

____

____

____

____

Think of words that you can use when you want to forgive someone who has hurt you.

____

____

____

LET US PRAY

O God, forgive us for times when we have hurt people. Teach us to be loving and kind to all we meet and to willingly offer forgiveness to others. Amen.

Benjamin • son of my right hand • Hebrew

8

Safe and Sound

READ
Exodus 1:22—2:10

After three months, she was not able to hide the baby any longer. So she got a basket and covered it with tar so that it would float. She put the baby in the basket. Then she put the basket among the tall grass at the edge of the Nile River. —Exodus 2:3 International Children's Bible

"Mew. Mew. Mew." Huddled together in a cardboard box in the shed, four tiny kittens called for their mother.

The black and white cat was out catching mice. But when she heard the kittens, she ran to them. In one leap, she jumped into the box and settled down to nurse them. The kittens felt warm, protected, and cared for.

Like house cats, wild animals choose a variety of places to cradle their young. Some baby animals live in dens, logs, nests, caves, rocks, trees, burrows, thickets, and even shallow dents in the ground. Tame animals, like cats and dogs, also have special places where they feel safe and like to sleep.

Baby Moses had a loving mother who wanted to keep him safe. She put him in a basket covered with tar to keep it from sinking. She placed the basket among the tall reeds along a river. This was her way of hiding the baby from harm. She also allowed him to be adopted because she knew Pharaoh's daughter would give the baby a good home.

Good mothers and fathers know how to keep their children safe. They find homes and food and clothing for their little ones. Good parents do many other things to keep their children comfortable and help them feel secure.

How do you feel cared for?

How do you know God cares for you?

Animals from A to Z

Match each animal with the name of its young. Answers are on page 209.

ape	baby
butterfly	bunny
deer	calf
eagle	caterpillar
frog	chick
goose	cub
kangaroo	eaglet
lion	fawn
monkey	foal
pig	gosling
quail	infant
rabbit	joey
sheep	lamb
turkey	piglet
viper	poult
yak	snakelet
zebra	tadpole

As kittens mew for their mothers, each of us cries to God.
—J.G.K.

LET US PRAY

Dear God and Parent of all, thank you for giving us parents who love and care for us. Thank you for everything they have done to give us places to live, food to eat, and clothing to wear. Keep caring for us as only you can. Amen.

9

ELEVATOR FRIENDS

READ
Exodus 3:1–5

God called to him out of the bush, "Moses, Moses!" And he said, "Here I am."
—Exodus 3:4

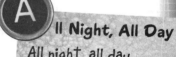

Elly and Sierra raced to the elevator in their apartment building. They lived at opposite ends of the hall and often saw each other as they left for school each morning. Elly got to the elevator first and pushed the call button. Sierra got there just as the doors slid open.

"Elly, can you come over after school?" Sierra asked as they rode down. "Grandma said I could ask. She's going to call your dad. You can eat with us too and see some of the changes we've made in our apartment. You just have to come! Please?"

It's fun to be invited to something. We get invitations to birthday parties or other special celebrations. We also are asked to eat everyday meals with friends or family. Whatever the reason, the person asking us to come over wants to spend time with us.

Moses was on a mountain when God's special invitation came to him. First, Moses saw a fiery bush, but the fire was not burning up the bush. From out of the bush God called to Moses and gave him instructions for how to lead the people. Throughout his life, Moses heard God's call to do special things, and Moses obeyed.

God gives us invitations too. Again and again, we hear an invitation to spend time with God, and follow God's way. God hopes we respond by saying, "Yes, Lord, I want to be very close to you always."

Today as we worship, let's accept God's invitation to come and enjoy God's friendship forever.

All Night, All Day

All night, all day,
Angels watchin' over me, my Lord;
All night, all day,
Angels watchin' over me.
—Spiritual

Where do you like to be with God?

When has God given you an invitation?

To Go to Heaven*

The God who loves us as no one other
has sent us Jesus to be our brother.
The way is Jesus. He changes never.
The Savior wants you with him forever.
—from Swahili song translated
by Howard S. Olson

LET US PRAY

Thank you, dear God, for inviting me to be close to you. I want to accept your call, and I want to tell you what a great and wonderful God you are. In your holy name, I pray. Amen.

Elly (Eleanor) • light • Greek

Sierra • mountain, black • Spanish

10

Newspaper Route

READ
Exodus 4:10–16

Do all things without murmuring and arguing.
—Philippians 2:14

"Do I have to help with the newspaper route tomorrow?" Lance asked after he'd spent all evening on homework. "Can't you do it by yourself this time?"

Lance's dad hesitated. "You agreed that if we took this job together, you'd help with it. This is the third time this week you're wanting out," he said.

"Yeah, but I had no idea that it would take up so much time," said Lance. "Besides, I'm not good at it anyway. You can do it so much faster if you drive than if I go on my bike."

"But if I throw the papers, you might miss out on the fun," his dad said.

Like Lance, Moses did not want to do his job. He told God that he was a poor speaker, and God promised to tell Moses what to say. Moses begged again. "Please send someone else," he said.

Serving God and other people is not always easy. At times, it takes lots of time and energy and abilities that we may think we don't have. Sometimes we just get so tired of doing the work that we want out. But, as Moses learned, God can help us in one way or another.

How does God want you to help others today? You don't want to miss out on the joy and fun of just doing it. With God's help, you can do it!

TO DO
- sweep bedrooms
- feed the cats
- practice violin
- wash dishes
- bake cookies

How do you think Lance and his dad settled their problem?

Tell about a time when you enjoyed helping someone.

Work

(mean voice)
I can't do the work.
I'm glued to my chair.
If I move from this spot,
I'll turn into a bear.

I can't help you paint.
I can't help you cook.
I can't help you clean.
I can't help you look.

There's only one way
I might help you today
And that's if you give me
a good bit of pay.
(pause)

(kind voice)
You've just changed my mind.
I'll help you indeed.
I'll help in the garden
and pull every weed.

I can help you paint.
I can help you cook.
I can help you clean.
I can help you look.

Forget what I said.
You don't have to remind.
I'll help you today.
I'll help humankind!
—J.G.K.

LET US PRAY.

Dear Lord, when we are tempted to complain about the work you want us to do, please help us. Remind us that service to others is service to you. In Jesus' name, we pray. Amen.

Lance (Lancelot) • attendant • English

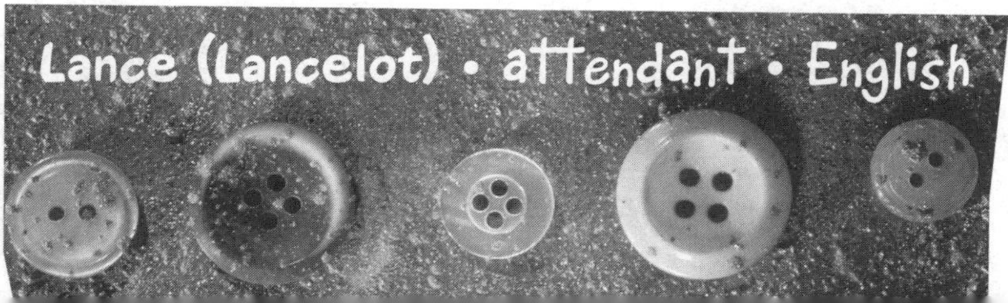

11

READ
Exodus 13:18, 21–22

The LORD will guide you continually.
—Isaiah 58:11a

First Ride

Danny could hardly sit still. For a long time he had waited for his first ride in an airplane, and today was the day. As he sat with his mommy, waiting to board the plane, he had lots of questions.

"When do we leave, Mommy?" Danny asked. "When do we get on the plane? How do the pilots see in the clouds? How do they know how to make the plane go up?" His mommy answered each question.

Danny stood by the window a long time and then asked his mommy, "Will God help the pilots when we are up in the air?"

"Yes, Danny. God will help us in the air and on the ground, here and there and all around," said Mommy, trying to sound like Dr. Seuss. Danny and his mommy laughed together at the sound of the rhyme.

Wherever we are, God is with us to guide us. In Exodus 13 we read about the way God guided the people as Moses led them out of Egypt. God sent a cloud and a fire so they knew where to go. God helped them find food and water, and gave them laws for living together.

In the Bible we read many stories about God's guidance and protection. Today, many years after Bible times, God still protects and guides us all the time.

What other stories remind you of God's guidance?

When have you felt God guiding you?

LET US PRAY

Dear Lord and Guide, we trust you to lead and help us no matter what we do or where we are. Amen.

Travel Prayer

In the air and on the ground,
Here and there and all around,
In the morning, noon, and night,
God will hold me very tight.

When I come and when I go,
When I'm fast and when I'm slow,
When I'm out and when I'm in,
God's with me through thick and thin.

When I give and when I take,
When I sleep and when I wake,
O dear Jesus, hear my prayer
For your guidance and your care.
—J.G.K.

Danny (Daniel) • God is my judge • Hebrew

12

Science Museum

READ Exodus 14:8-10, 15-16

Awesome is God in his sanctuary, the God of Israel; he gives power and strength to his people. Blessed be God! —Psalm 68:35

In the science museum, Pedro and his classmates looked at an exhibit on electricity. They tried experiments that showed static electricity. They pushed buttons that created miniature lightning. They learned about switches and circuits and magnets.

"What is electricity?" Pedro asked his teacher. "I don't understand."

"Electricity is a force that we can't see. We can only see what electricity does," the teacher said. She told him about light bulbs and electric machines and microphones and stereos. We can see all those things, she said, but we can't see the power that makes them work.

"Is electricity like God?" Pedro asked.

Like Pedro, we have a hard time understanding this magnificent world and the all-powerful God who created it. We can't see God, but we do see all kinds of wonderful things that God's power has caused.

With great power, God made the earth. With great power, God gives strength to weak and tired people. With great power, God rules forever.

Like Moses and others throughout history, we know that our God is a reliable source of power for us. We know we can trust God to take care of us.

What one thing that requires batteries or electricity for power reminds you of God? (Example: God is like a radio because God speaks to me.)

What is something in creation that tells you God is powerful?

Awesome God

Our God is an awesome God.
He reigns from heaven above
In wisdom, power and love.
Our God is an awesome God.
—Rich Mullins

LET US PRAY

Almighty God, we thank you that you are the source of all power. We thank you that your power will last forever. We thank you for ways that you use your great power to help us. Amen.

Our Lord is great and very powerful. There is no limit to what he knows.
—Psalm 147:5
International Children's Bible

13

Big Complaints

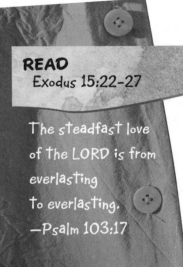

READ
Exodus 15:22-27

The steadfast love of the LORD is from everlasting to everlasting.
—Psalm 103:17

At the baseball game, Brooke watched as people ate nachos.

"Can I have money to buy some nachos?" Brooke begged. She'd already had several snacks and wasn't surprised when her mother said to wait until they got home. But Brooke couldn't wait.

"I'm hungry. I'm thirsty. I'm hot. I'm tired. I want some nachos right now!" she announced.

After three days in the wilderness, Moses and the people he had led out of Egypt were still looking for water.

"What will we drink? What will we drink?" they demanded. And when they did find water, it tasted so bad they couldn't drink it.

This wasn't the only time they complained. Even after God had led them to find water they could drink, the people still complained as they journeyed through the wilderness. They wanted better food. They feared for their safety. They didn't like the decisions their leaders made.

We too find reasons to complain even when we have what we need. Complaining is the easy way to react to a problem.

But this story reminds us that even when we complain, God cares for us. God leads us to find what we really need. Like the poet says in Psalm 103:17, God's love is "from everlasting to everlasting." That's forever! Thanks, God!

Do you ever complain?

How does God provide for your needs?

LET US PRAY

Forgive us, Lord, for times when we complain about little things that bother us. Thank you for caring for us and for providing us with good food and water. Teach us to be patient when we have to wait. In your holy name, we pray. Amen.

Complaining

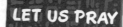

I stepped upon a wad of gum
when I was at the rink,
a huge and sticky wad of gum
that didn't want to shrink.

I started to complain about
the one who left this mess,
"How dumb of you to leave it there!"
I muttered, more or less.

Then I recalled that earlier,
when I was at the rink,
A chewy goo fell from my mouth,
Pink bubblegum, I think.

—J.G.K.

Brooke • brook • English

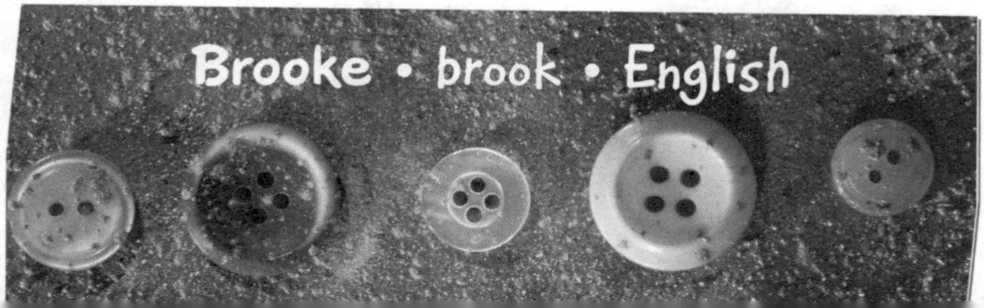

14

Heavenly Corn

READ
Exodus 16:31-35

My God will fully satisfy every need of yours according to his riches in glory in Christ Jesus.
—Philippians 4:19

"Amazing! Truly amazing!" Jaden couldn't believe what he had read. "Hey, everyone, listen up. Did you know that corn has an incredibly long shelf life?"

"What does that mean?" asked his sister Talia.

"It can last a long time. Scientists have been able to pop corn that's a thousand years old!"

"Cool," said Talia. "I wonder what it tasted like. Does salt and butter last that long too?"

Some foods, especially those that are dried or canned, can last a long time and still be good to eat. Others last only a short time.

After the Hebrews left Egypt, they ate a food called manna. Manna lasted only one day. Each night God provided the manna in an amount that was just right for the number of people it would serve the next day.

Other Bible passages call manna *corn from heaven* or *bread from heaven* or *angels' bread*. Jesus even called himself manna when he said, "I am the bread of life."

Just as God gave the Israelites the food they needed, so God gives us just what we need to live. Each day God serves us, teaching us how to use what we have to bless others.

Why did God give the people manna instead of other food?

What gifts do we have from God that last only a short time?

God Loves a Picnic*

The people fled from Egypt, yes they did
The people fled from Egypt, yes they did
They wandered in the desert, yes they did
And God gave them a picnic.

Our God loves a picnic, yes God does
God loves a picnic, yes God does
God loves a picnic, yes God does
Let's all go to the picnic!
—Bryan Moyer Suderman

LET US PRAY

Dear God, thank you for taking care of all our needs. Thank you for food. Thank you for homes. Thank you that we can use what we have to bless others today. Amen.

Jaden • God has heard • Hebrew

Talia • dew from heaven • Hebrew

15

READ
Exodus 20:8-11

Six days you shall work, but on the seventh day you shall rest; even in plowing time and in harvest time you shall rest.
—Exodus 34:21

Voice Vacation

Fog hung over the park as Nisha's family followed the paths on a family walk before church. They heard a plane fly far overhead, but they couldn't see it because of the fog.

Dad suggested that since they couldn't see well, they should listen extra hard. "No talking for five minutes," he said. "How many sounds can we hear?"

At first Nisha heard only their footsteps. Then she tuned in to the sounds around her. Birds warbled, a dog barked, a train tooted, the creek babbled, geese honked, cars hummed. When Nisha stopped walking, she heard gentle drops of water fall from the tree branches, hitting wet leaves below.

When we take a vacation from our voices, we can hear all kinds of sounds. When we take time off in our busy lives, as the Ten Commandments tell us to, we are often surprised by what is around us. Even when our busy schedules tell us to work, it's important to rest regularly. Rest and renewal give us a chance to hear God speaking to us.

Q

What sounds from nature have surprised you recently?

How do you honor God's day of rest?

This Is the Day*

This is the day, this is the day,
That the Lord has made, that the Lord has made.
We will rejoice. we will rejoice,
And be glad in it, and be glad in it.
This is the day that the Lord has made,
We will rejoice and be glad in it!
This is the day, this is the day
That the Lord has made.

—Words from Psalm 118:24;
arrangement © Scripture in Song

LET US PRAY.

Dear God, when you made the world, you set aside one day for rest. Help us to honor you as we celebrate your Lord's Day. As we rest from work, help us tune in to you. Amen.

Nisha • night • Hindi

16

You First

"You go first," Reece said to Tyler.

"No, you," Tyler replied.

Tyler's mother had given them clear instructions to take some newly picked grapes to the neighbors. But the boys didn't really want to do it.

Between Tyler's house and the one next door, they stopped. Loaded down with baskets of grapes, they still felt nervous. But then they saw their neighbor smiling at them and welcoming them. Suddenly they weren't nervous any more.

"Thank you. Thank you," she said before Reece and Tyler could give her the fruit.

It's easy for us to think of reasons not to do what we know is right. We think we're too tired, too young, too busy, or too weak. We think we don't know how to do what we're being asked to do. We might be afraid we will get hurt. We might think we don't have enough money.

But when we make even the smallest effort, God rewards us for trying.

In the Bible we read about Caleb, who served God with his whole heart. He wanted to follow God's way completely, and he knew he could do what God expected of him. While others hesitated to follow God's direction, Caleb did what he was asked to do.

He told the people, "The Lord is with us. Don't be afraid." Caleb knew how great God was. Caleb had the courage to obey God even when others didn't.

Now be quiet with God and listen for guidance. Then promise to serve God with your whole heart.

READ
Numbers 14:20-24

Do not rebel against the LORD; . . . the LORD is with us.
—Numbers 14:9

What excuses do you often use for not doing the right thing?

What good things happen when you serve Jesus wholeheartedly?

If you want happiness for an hour, take a nap.
If you want happiness for a day, go fishing.
If you want happiness for a year, inherit a fortune.
If you want happiness for a lifetime, help somebody.
—Chinese proverb

LET US PRAY

Dear God, help me to accept your plans for my life. Help me to serve you with my whole heart today and every day. Amen.

Reece • enthusiastic, stream • English
Tyler • tile maker • English

17

READ
Numbers 27:15-19, 22-23

Serve one another with whatever gift each of you has received.
—1 Peter 4:10

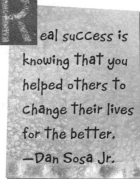

Real success is knowing that you helped others to change their lives for the better.
—Dan Sosa Jr.

Construction

Von and his friends were pretending they were building a skyscraper.

"I'm driving the bulldozer," Von said.

"I'm operating the crane," said William.

"I'm pouring cement," said Ren.

"I'm the construction manager," said Dakota. "You might think construction manager doesn't sound big, but it is. My mom said so."

All jobs are important. Each one needs people with special abilities. Construction workers, like bulldozer drivers and cement pourers, need to know how to work with materials and equipment so that the buildings they make are safe and last a long time. The construction manager listens to the person who wants the building built and then organizes the work and the workers so that the job gets done.

Joshua was like a construction manager for God. God knew Joshua had the talent to lead the people after Moses could no longer do the work. Joshua got his instructions from God and became a good leader.

Like Joshua, all of us have received skills and talents from God. God wants us to use these gifts to serve other people in our homes, churches, and communities. We appreciate those who lead and teach and help us. But God has given all of us different skills so that we can live and work together, helping each other and serving God with our talents.

Jobs are important, but the best and most important work we can do is to serve and follow God.

What kind of job would you like to have some day?

Name several people you can help this week.

LET US PRAY.

Dear God, thank you for giving us good people to lead and help us. Guide them as they share your love. Bless and protect them in their work for you. Help them to be good examples, and may they be happy in serving you. Be with all of us this day. We pray this in Jesus' name. Amen.

Dakota • friend, partner • Dakota (Native American)
Ren • arranger • Japenese
Von • from (the family of) • German
William • protector • English

18

READ
Deuteronomy
5:6-22

Your statutes [commandments] have been my songs wherever I make my home.
—Psalm 119:54

ONE THREE TWO

Listen as I count to ten. One, three, six, four, nine, two, eight, five, seven, ten. Is that right? No, of course not. Numbers are supposed to be in order. When they're mixed up, we get confused.

God understands that most of us like to live our lives in a way that is orderly and easy to understand. That's one reason God gave us the Ten Commandments. God doesn't make us follow these laws; God wants us to follow them because we want to and because they make sense. God gave them to us to help us understand how best to live with God and with other people. The Ten Commandments also tell us about what is important to God (Exodus 20:1-17, Deuteronomy 5:6-21).

Moses taught the people to follow the Lord's instructions so that they would be happy in life (Deuteronomy 5:33). When we follow God's rules for living, we worship God with our lives. No wonder the psalmist wants to sing about God's instructions!

Jesus said that God's laws call us to love God and neighbor (Matthew 22:37-40). As you worship today, name and count reasons why it's good to have God and the Ten Commandments as guides to follow everyday.

How do the Ten Commandments help you understand God?

How do the Commandments help us live with others and God?

The Ten Commandments—a summary

No other gods. (Deuteronomy 6:6-7)
No idols. (8-10)
No vain use of God's name. (11)
Keep the Sabbath holy. (12-15)
Honor your father and mother. (16)
No murder. (17)
No adultery. (18)
No stealing. (19)
No false testimony. (20)
No coveting. (21)

Honor God and obey his commands. This is the most important thing people can do. —Ecclesiastes 12:13

LET US PRAY

Dear God, whose Commandments we want to follow, thank you for showing us how to live. Help us to honor you as we use your Ten Commandments to guide our actions. Amen.

19

READ
Deuteronomy 15:7-8, 10-11

Anyone who is kind to the needy honors God.
—Proverbs 14:31
International Children's Bible

Tightfist Day

Lula and her friends played a silly game at the community club where they often went after school.

"Today is tightfist day," the leader explained. "In everything you do today, you must grip your hands together in a fist. You're going to have to figure out how to do everything I ask, because your hands have to remain tightly closed."

The games started with Drop the Handkerchief and Charades. Then the group tried Wiffleball, a game something like softball but with a plastic ball and bat. Lula and the others tried a relay game where they picked up pennies, ran around a chair, and dropped them into an empty jar.

"Aren't our tight fists keeping us from what we're supposed to be doing?" Lula asked.

In real life, people who don't want to use their money are called tightfisted. They have a hard time sharing because they want to hold onto their money as long as they can.

The Bible encourages us to open our hands and give generously to people in need. God doesn't like it when there are people who are poor, sick, hungry, or hurting. Serving people in need is one way we honor God. Each time we are kind and give money, goods, or a helping hand to those in need, we are helping God.

There's only one time when we should be tightfisted, and that's when we're playing a game.

Try to seize two things, and one will always slip from your grasp! —Swahili proverb

What do you like to do with your hands?

How can you and your family open your hands to help people in your neighborhood?

LET US PRAY

O Lord and God, thank you for teaching us to share. Please guide us to be more willing to open our hands to help people in need. Amen.

IT IS MORE BLESSED TO GIVE THAN TO RECEIVE —Acts 20:35

20

I Can

READ

Judges 6:11-16a

The Lord said to Gideon, "I will be with you."
—Judges 6:16

"I can't," Drew said.

"Why not?" asked his stepmom.

"I really need you to go to the store for me."

He'd been to the store many times *with* his stepmom, but he didn't want to go alone. It was a big store. He might not be able to find all the items she wanted. He didn't want to have to look for all the things and he was worried about how to pay.

"I can't," he repeated. "I just can't."

We all have times when we think we can't do something. That's called self-doubt.

In today's Bible story we read about Gideon, whose self-doubt was a big problem. God sent an angel to Gideon because God wanted him to lead Israel.

No way! Gideon did not want to follow the angel's instructions. Gideon worried that God didn't care about him and his people. He complained that he was the youngest in his family and that his family was weak. But even though Gideon tried to get out of accepting God's call, he was still God's choice. Gideon learned to trust God.

We too can learn to trust God. We can change from saying, "No, I can't do that," to "Yes, Lord, I can!" We can trust God to give us confidence. We can do what God wants us to do.

If we promise to follow the way of Jesus, we might still wonder if we are the right person for God's work. Jesus understands our feelings, but he also gives us the strength to say, "Yes," to God's call.

What excuses do you often use when you are asked to do a job?

Why does God promise to take care of us?

Go Now in Peace*

Go now in peace,
go now in peace,
may the love of God surround you
ev'rywhere, ev'rywhere
you may go.

—Natalie Sleeth

LET US PRAY

Dear God, even when we are weak and feel small, we know you are God and we trust you to care for us. Amen.

Drew (Andrew) • Courageous • Greek

21

Bethlehem Bread

READ
Ruth 1:22–2:7

Serve one another with whatever gift each of you has received.
—1 Peter 4:10

In the fairy tale, "Hansel and Gretel," a poor family worries because they don't have enough food. When Gretel starts to cry, her brother, Hansel, tells her, "Don't worry, Gretel, I will take care of you, and God will not leave us."

On a walk into the forest, the two children leave a trail of bread crumbs, but birds eat the crumbs, and Hansel and Gretel can't find their way home.

"Dear God, please help us," the children pray. By the end of the story, Hansel and Gretel are no longer lost. They have found their father and food.

Have you ever been really hungry, or not had enough money to buy food? Have you ever been lost?

In today's Bible story we read about Naomi and Ruth. Naomi had left her home in Bethlehem because there wasn't enough food there.

Years later, she moved back to Bethlehem with her daughter-in-law Ruth at the time when barley was being harvested. Barley was used to make bread, especially during times when there wasn't enough rain for crops to grow. In Bethlehem, Naomi and Ruth found a good home.

Bread and other kinds of food help us grow and keep us from being hungry. When we have enough to eat, we know God cares for us. At the same time, we can remember to ask God to take care of others who may be in need.

What is your favorite kind of bread?

The word Bethlehem means house of bread. What name could you give to your own home that would help others know it is a special place for God?

Choose to earn your bread
by the labor of your hands,
and to eat your bread with peace.

—Soetgen van den Houte,
a 16th-century Belgian martyr,
in a letter to her children

LET US PRAY.

God is great and God is good
And we thank you for our food.
By your hand we all are fed.
Give us, Lord, our daily bread.
Amen.

Hansel (Hans) • the Lord is gracious • **German**

Gretel (Margaret) • pearl • Greek

22

READ
1 Samuel 3:1-10; 19-20

The LORD came and stood there, calling as before, "Samuel! Samuel!" And Samuel said, "Speak, for your servant is listening."
—1 Samuel 3:10

What's Your Name?

"Justin, Justin, why aren't you responding?" his mom whispered just so Justin could hear. "This woman is talking to you, and you're standing there not saying anything to her. She'll think you're being rude."

Justin whispered back. "I didn't know she was talking to me. Besides, I can't understand her. I heard her talking, but her speaking is different from ours. What did she ask?"

"She wants to know your name."

Justin listened again to the woman they'd met in the store. Every word sounded different from the way his mom spoke, but finally he understood the woman. "My name is Justin. What's yours?"

Sometimes we don't understand what's going on. We don't know what words mean, we don't hear very well, or we can't understand another person's accent or language. When that happens, we don't know what to think.

Samuel was like that. He was a boy, serving Eli in the temple. One night God called Samuel, and Samuel didn't know how to respond. He kept going to Eli to help him understand what he was hearing.

In that nighttime visit God called Samuel to be a judge, a prophet, and a priest. Samuel accepted this call and faithfully followed the Lord throughout his life.

Sometimes God talks to us. If we don't know it is God, we don't know how to respond. Others who have heard God speak to them can help us, just like Eli helped Samuel. Often, we need someone to help us hear God speaking. Like Samuel, we too can answer God by obeying God's voice.

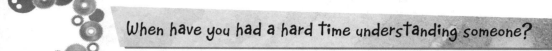

When have you had a hard time understanding someone?

Who has helped you know God and to listen to God's voice?

Jesus, You Have Called Us*

LAOTIAN:
Pah Jesu song ern kha
Bo kheuy jak hang hern
Kho serm kam lang
Hai kha tam pai.

ENGLISH:
Jesus, you have called us;
you will never leave us.
Give us the strength
to follow you.
—Doug and Jude Krehbiel

LET US PRAY

Dear God, who called Samuel, speak to us so that we can hear you. As you have guided your people through many years, guide us today. Amen.

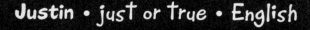

Justin • just or true • English

23

READ
1 Kings 8:22-23

I am your servant, and you are the LORD my God. Hear this prayer I am praying to you today.
—1 Kings 8:28 International Children's Bible

Prayer Glove

Gloves. How many different kinds of gloves can you name? *(Allow time for responses.)* Did you think of these: wool, rubber, garden, dress, baseball, ski, driving, disposable, surgical, and industrial gloves.

When we wear gloves, they keep our hands clean, or they help protect our hands from injury. Just as there are many kinds of gloves, there are also many kinds of prayers.

Let's imagine that the gloves we wear are "prayer gloves." When we wear them, they help us feel connected to God. They prepare us for the work God has for us. They connect us to others who pray to God.

In today's Bible reading, King Solomon said a prayer of dedication for the temple. What other kinds of prayers can you name? *(Allow time for responses. Examples could include table graces and bedtime prayers, the Lord's Prayer, or prayers of thanks.)*

We pray to give praise and glory to God. We give thanks for God's goodness to us. We ask for forgiveness and for the willingness to forgive others. We pray prayers for ourselves and for other people.

When you pray, think of yourself holding hands with God.

Q

Do you have a favorite prayer you like to say?

Use paper and pencil to trace around your hand to make a paper prayer glove. On it list names of people for whom you want to remember to pray.

God shapes the world by prayer.
The more praying there is in the world,
the better the world will be.
—E. M. Bounds

LET US PRAY

Before we close our devotional time, let's take time for silent prayer. Hold your prayer glove, point to each finger, and say a silent prayer for someone else.

(Sit in silence for a few moments.)

For our prayer we are going to pray Psalm 19:14. I will say a few words and you repeat after me:

Let the words of my mouth
ALL: LET THE WORDS OF MY MOUTH
and the meditation of my heart
ALL: AND THE MEDITATION OF MY HEART
be acceptable to you,
ALL: BE ACCEPTABLE TO YOU,
O Lord, my rock and my redeemer.
ALL: O LORD, MY ROCK AND MY REDEEMER.
Amen.
ALL: AMEN.

24

Prays–Praise

READ
Psalm 47:1, 5–9

Sing praises to God, sing praises; sing praises to our King, sing praises.
—Psalm 47:6

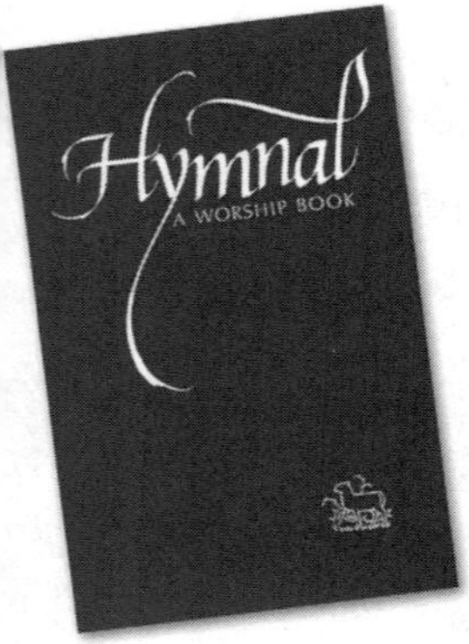

"How many 'prays' are there?" JoJo asked after choir practice at church.

His older sister was confused. "What do you mean?" she asked.

"Well," JoJo said. "There are p-r-a-i-s-e and p-r-a-y-s and p-r-e-y-s and even a word in the dictionary that is p-r-a-s-e. I don't understand that one at all. When we praise God, are we really praying to God? The words sound the same to me."

Are you like JoJo? Do you sometimes wonder what it means to praise God?

Today's reading from Psalm 47 is a joyful song. In verse six alone we read "sing praises" four times! These are joyful and sincere words that say "thank you" to our God.

When we are happy, we want to share our good news. It is really good news when we join with people all over the earth to sing that God rules over us all.

As we praise and glorify God with our shouts and our clapping, our instruments and our voices, let us remember to pray to God with our hearts. That's not confusing!

What words mean the same as "praise"?

When you pray, how often do you praise God at the same time?

Praise God from Whom All Blessings Flow*

KOREAN:

Manboke keunwon hananim
on bakseong chansong drigo
Jeo cheonsayeo chansonghasei,
chansong seongbu, seogja, seongryoung.

ENGLISH:

Praise God from whom all blessings flow;
praise him all creatures here below;
praise him above ye heav'nly host;
praise Father, Son, and Holy Ghost. Amen.

—Thomas Ken

LET US PRAY

We praise you, O God, because you are a great and awesome ruler. You reign over us and everyone in this big wide world. We praise you for being our God. Amen.

For centuries, Christians have sung Psalm 47 on Ascension Day, the day we remember when Jesus returned to heaven (Acts 1:6-11).

JoJo (Joseph) • God will increase • Hebrew

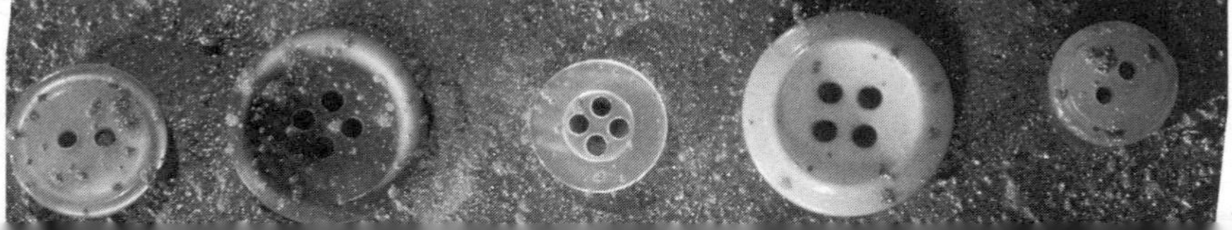

25

To Worship

(To the leader: Hand out paper and drawing supplies before you begin. Explain that as you read, the worshippers may draw pictures of what worship looks like. Ask, "How do you like to worship? How do you feel when you worship God?")

Felicia was traveling with her cousins and aunt and uncle to visit friends. They talked about their plans for the weekend together. They were going to swim in the ocean, visit museums, and hike in the forest.

"Are we going to go to church?" Felicia asked. "I don't want to miss Sunday school." Church was important to her. She felt good when she worshipped and sang with others and learned about God.

"We'll go with our friends to their church," her uncle said. "We can worship God anywhere."

The poet who wrote Psalm 84 loved going to God's temple. The temple was in Jerusalem where people traveled for special religious festivals. The psalmist was even a little jealous of the birds that built their nests inside the temple's walls. They could be in the temple all the time!

Each of us has a special place where we feel God close to us. It may be our church building or a place in our home where we worship. But the place isn't as important as just being with God. We can be close to God anytime because God's Spirit lives within us—wherever we are.

READ
Psalm 84:1-4

You yourselves are God's temple. God's Spirit lives in you.
—1 Corinthians 3:16
International Children's Bible

Where do you go to feel God close to you?

How do you know God's Spirit is living in you?

LET US PRAY

O Lord God, I am happy when I am with you. Thank you for my church building and other special places where I worship you. And thank you that I can be with you anywhere, anytime. Amen.

ADULT TIP: Take God with you on vacation

- Plan ahead. Take the initiative to plan for worship. Pack Bible, devotional readings, and hymnbooks. Learn worship times for churches where you plan to visit.
- Lead family worship the first day—with prayer, song, Bible reading, song and prayer. Keep it simple.
- Read aloud passages from the book of Acts to learn about Paul's travels.
- Visit cathedrals and other places of worship.
- Memorize Bible passages as you travel.
- Make up songs or new verses to favorite tunes as a way to thank God for your experiences.
- Look for Christian symbols, such doves or crosses. Photograph them or keep a written record of them.
- When you are in a crowd and don't want to bother other travelers, pass a sheet of paper to each family member. Ask everyone to draw or write a prayer. Use them later in a worship time.
- Make daily quiet time a part of the vacation.

Felicia • happiness • Latin

26

READ
Psalm 104:24-30

Look at the sea,
so big and wide.
Its creatures large
and small cannot
be counted.
—Psalm 104:25
International
Children's Bible

A Monster!

"It's a monster!" squealed Devon. "Help! Help!" His dream had been so real that even after Devon awoke, he was still scared. He remembered big teeth and a huge jaw.

The next morning at breakfast his family talked about monsters. "They're not real. Get over it," chided his older brother, not sounding very sympathetic.

"But it was real," Devon said.

Monsters and scary things can seem very real even if we just imagine them or dream about them. Sea monsters are mentioned several times in the Bible. Some versions of the Bible call them *leviathans*, a word we don't quite understand. In the psalm we read today, the poet describes the leviathan as a creature God made to play in the ocean. It might have been a whale or a dolphin.

God's world is full of many things we don't understand and even some things we are afraid of. If we learn about things we don't understand, and if we realize that God made all creatures, we often discover that we no longer have to be afraid of them.

What things frighten you?

How can God help you deal with the monsters you imagine?

Fears

O God, you can help me not be afraid
'cause creatures I fear
are things you have made:

The BIRD that flies close,
the SPIDER I see,
the THUNDER that booms,
the DOG that runs free,
the CAT with sharp claws,
the SNAKE that can sneak,
the WATER that swirls,
the MOUSE that says, "Squeak."

Please help me, dear God, to cheer, not to fear,
each creature you've made, each thing you hold dear.
—J.G.K.

LET US PRAY

In your wisdom, O God, you made many wonderful creatures, including many we don't understand. Thank you that we can learn more and more about your creation. Help us not be afraid of it. Amen.

27

Sun Tent

READ
Psalm 136:1-9, 26

(Leader reads first part of each verse; worshippers repeat: "for his steadfast love endures forever.")

The setting sun was reflected in the calm water of the lake, all bathed in reds and oranges. As Ilona and other campers fished, they chatted about the sun's size, its age and temperature, its distance from earth, and the times of sunrise and sunset.

Later, around their campfire, the sparks and the glowing wood pieces reminded them of the sun's color. Their camping leader read from Psalm 19.

"Why do you think the psalmist says, 'In the heavens God has set a tent for the sun?'" the leader asked.

"Is it because God couldn't decide where to set up the tent?" Ilona asked.

Even though we know that the earth rotates around the sun, to us on earth the sun looks like it is always moving—just like nomads, people who live in tents and keep setting up new camps.

We know from the Bible that God made the sun and that it and all creation are under God's control. We know too that the sun marks the days and the seasons and tells us directions by its rising and setting. The heavens tell about how wonderful God is.

God made the great big sun and created a home for it in the sky. We know that God cares for us, too. God has given us the great big earth for our home.

Praise God!

The heavens are telling the glory of God.... In the heavens he has set a tent for the sun.
—Psalm 19:1, 4

What part of the sky is your favorite?

What makes your home a good place to live?

Our Sun: True or False

Which of these statements are true? (Answers are on page 209.)

- God made the sun.
- The sun is really a star.
- Our earth goes around the sun.
- The sun gives the earth light and heat.
- The sun is 93 million miles from earth.
- It takes light eight-and-a-half minutes to travel from the sun to the earth.
- The sun is so big that more than one million earths could fit inside it.

Praise him, sun and moon; praise him, all you shining stars!
—Psalm 148:3

Sun Prayer

For the sun that lights each day
  Lord, I thank you as I pray.
For the dark, the stars and moon,
  For the sunrise, morn and noon,
For the glow of sun up high,
  And the big majestic sky,
For the shadows and the shade,
  And the evening's easy fade.
For each day that follows night,
  For the good that comes from light,
For the sun and heaven's glow
  As it reaches us below,
For the sun that lights each day,
Lord, I thank you as I pray.
—J.G.K.

Ilona • sunshine • Hungarian

28

READ
Psalm 148

Young men and women alike, old and young together! Let them praise the name of the LORD. —Psalm 148:12-13a

Praise God!

"Hey, Sunshine, I'm so glad to see you!" The old man's eyes sparkled as Miranda gave him a hymnbook.

Today was Saturday and Miranda was at the retirement center where her mom led a sing-along. The man always called Miranda "Sunshine," but that was okay. She liked to think of herself as bringing sunshine into others' lives.

Sometimes Miranda would make decorations or serve refreshments. She liked to talk with the residents. Whenever they saw her, they would smile and tell her stories from their childhood.

More than anything, Miranda liked to sing along during worship. Some of the people knew every word to every verse of every hymn.

Psalm 148 is a song that calls everyone and everything to praise God. All of us in heaven and on earth, old and young, are called to praise the Lord. According to verse 12, we are to do it together.

Imagine worshipping with everything in creation—not just by ourselves in our own bedrooms, not just with our family or church, but with all creation together! What a party of praise that would be!

Our prayers and praises, says the psalm, are very much like the prayers of the angels or the praises of all creation. Whoever and wherever we are, let's praise God.

Who are some of your favorite people—old and young?

What activities do you like to do to help people in your community?

Now Thank We All Our God*

Now thank we all our God with heart and hands and voices,
who wondrous things has done, in whom this world rejoices,
who, from our mothers' arms, has blessed us on our way
with countless gifts of love, and still is ours today.

All praise and thanks to God the Father now be given,
the Son, and him who reigns with them in highest heaven—
the one eternal God, whom earth and heav'n adore,
for thus it was, is now, and shall be evermore.

—Martin Rinckart

LET US PRAY.

Praise to you, Lord God, who created the heavens and the earth. Help us to know how we can live together, sharing our lives with those older and younger than we are. Amen.

29

New Trumpet

READ
Psalm 150

Praise him with trumpet sound . . . Let everything that breathes praise the LORD. Praise the LORD! —Psalm 150:3a, 6

After his first trumpet lesson Jordan felt his lips. They were still tingling as he sat down with his family for supper. His lips remembered every blow he had forced through them. But he was excited. For a long time he had waited to get his trumpet, and now he was learning to play it.

Before the meal, Jordan's dad read from Psalm 150. He came to verse three, which says, "Praise God with trumpet sound."

Jordan's ears perked up, and without thinking, he interrupted his dad. "There's a trumpet in the Bible! I didn't know that. I'm playing an instrument that's in the Bible! That's cool!"

Our ears perk up when we hear musical instruments. We like the sounds they make and are amazed when good musicians play so well.

In Bible times there were three kinds of instruments—ones that you hit, such as tamborines, and cymbals; ones that you blew into, like pipes, flutes, and ram's horns; and ones that had strings, such as harps, lyres, and guitars.

The word *psalm* means a hymn accompanied by stringed instruments. During the time of King David, singers and musicians often led worship (1 Chronicles 15:16). They sang from the Book of Psalms, which is the oldest book of songs still used in worship.

The poet who wrote Psalm 150 tells everything that breathes to "praise the Lord." Praising God is as simple as breathing.

As every breath of air leaves our mouths, so does our praise to God. Each day of our lives, we can make music and offer praise to our Lord.

What is your favorite kind of musical instrument?

Why does God like the music we make during worship?

Praise poem

Each morning when I wake,
With every breath I take,
With every sound I make,
To Jesus I give praise.
—J.G.K.

LET US PRAY

We praise you, Lord, Creator of song and music. We thank you for tuning our hearts to sing your praise. Hallelujah! Hallelujah! Amen.

Jordan • descendant • Hebrew

30

Buried Treasure

READ
Proverbs 2:1–5

The LORD gives wisdom; from his mouth come knowledge and understanding.
—Proverbs 2:6

In Mark Twain's book, *The Adventures of Tom Sawyer*, Tom and his friend Huck set out to find buried treasure. Huck didn't understand why anyone would want to bury money when it could be spent, but Tom convinced his friend that treasures could be found almost anywhere.

"Say, Huck, if we find a treasure here, what [are] you going to do with your share?" asked Tom.

"Well, I'll have pie and a glass of soda every day, and I'll go to every circus that comes along," said Huck.

What would you do if you found buried treasure?

One kind of treasure that we can all search for is wisdom. But finding it can be even more difficult than finding buried treasure.

What is wisdom? It's the ability to know what is right and to make good choices. If we make those choices by trusting God to help us rather than relying only on ourselves, then we are truly wise.

The book of Proverbs contains 915 sayings, most of them from King Solomon. These proverbs are based on the idea that the "fear of the Lord" is the beginning of wisdom.

Fearing the Lord does not mean we are afraid of God. It means we respect and worship God and follow God's ways. When we are close to God, loving God and knowing that God loves us, we are wise. This is the greatest treasure we could ever find.

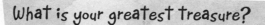

What is your greatest treasure?

When will you need God's special wisdom today?

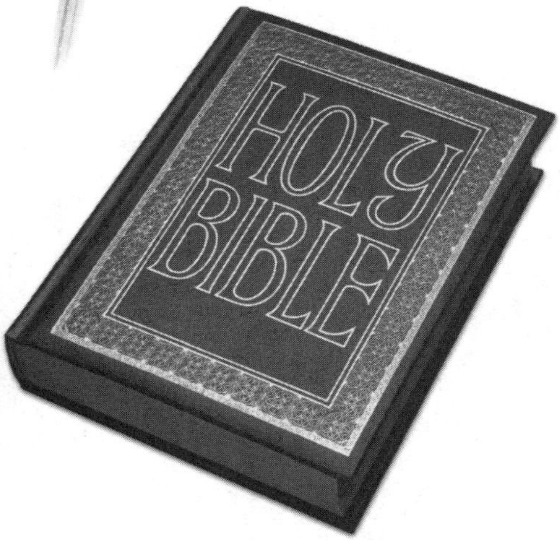

The greatest wisdom of all is kindness.
—Hebrew proverb

LET US PRAY

Wise God, we come to you for the wisdom we need. As we honor you with our lives, we trust you to help us know how to make the right choices each day. Amen.

Tom (Thomas) – a twin – Greek

Huck (Huckleberry) – a fruit; a term of affection for a friend – American English

31

Locked In

READ
Proverbs 3:5-8

Trust in the LORD with all your heart, and do not rely on your own insight.
—Proverbs 3:5

Mariah gasped. She thought she knew how to unlock the bathroom door, but now it wouldn't open. She was going to yell for help, but just as she opened her mouth, she remembered something her Sunday school teacher had once told her: "When you're in a snare, say a little prayer."

Taking a big breath, Mariah closed her eyes and said, "Please, God, I need help unlocking the door." After a moment she began to relax.

Then she heard a voice on the other side of the door, "Do you need help?"

"Yes, please," Mariah responded. "I'm locked in."

Proverbs is a book of poems and sayings that teach us how to be wise. The most important truth it teaches is that we must learn to trust God. That's a big challenge for each of us, whatever our age. We all like to think we can do things by ourselves. We don't want anyone telling us what to do or say.

God is far wiser than we humans will ever be. When we allow ourselves to lean on God, only then are we really wise. God is the key to true wisdom.

Tell about a time when you were stuck and tried to solve a problem through your own wisdom.

How can we help each other "trust in the Lord with all [our] heart"?

When We Walk with the Lord*

When we walk with the Lord,
in the light of his word,
what a glory he sheds on our way!
While we do his good will,
he abides with us still,
and with all who will trust and obey.

Trust and obey,
for there's no other way
to be happy in Jesus,
but to trust and obey.

Then in fellowship sweet,
we will sit at his feet,
or we'll walk by his side in the way.
What he says, we will do,
where he sends we will go,
never fear, only trust and obey. —John H. Samms

LET US PRAY

Dear Lord God, you are wiser than everyone on earth. We ask for wisdom. Help us to learn to trust you rather than only ourselves. Amen.

Miranda • wonderful, admirable • Latin

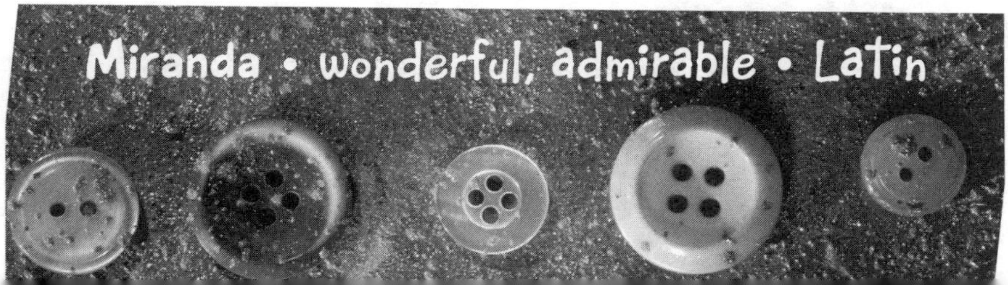

32

It's Time

READ
Ecclesiastes 3:1-8

For everything there is a season, and a time for every matter under heaven.
—Ecclesiastes 3:1

With only pages to read in his book, Alex jolted into the present. He hadn't heard Gramps call the first time. "Time for your bath and bed," Gramps yelled. "There's no time like the present! Get in here!"

Alex ran towards the shower where Gramps waited. "I wish I could finish the last chapter before I go to sleep," Alex said as he got out of his clothes. "This book is cool. It's about time travel. Gramps, do you ever wonder what it would be like to live in the 23rd century?"

"No, Alex, I don't usually think about that," Gramps replied with a grin. "But I do sometimes think about tomorrow!"

Books, movies, and hobbies have a way of making time stand still for us. We can get so absorbed in them that we forget to live in the present.

"For everything there is a season," says the teacher who wrote the book of Ecclesiastes. Like the seasons of spring, summer, fall, and winter, some parts of our lives repeat themselves. We get up in the morning, work and play in the day, and go to bed at night. Every morning we get up, and every night we go to bed.

These verses remind us that God sets the times for life's rhythms. We don't have to worry about when things will happen. We know that God takes care of the seasons of our lives, and we can be thankful for that!

Which activities do you like so much that you lose track of time?

What season do you enjoy the most?

Everything in Its Time

For everything there is a season, and
a time for every matter under heaven:
a time to be born, and a time to die;
a time to plant,
and a time to pluck up what is planted;
a time to kill,
and a time to heal,
a time to break down,
and a time to build up;
a time to weep,
and a time to laugh;
a time to mourn,
and a time to dance;
a time to throw away stones,
and a time to gather stones together;
a time to embrace,
and a time to refrain from embracing;
a time to seek, and a time to lose;
a time to keep,
and a time to throw away;
a time to tear,
and a time to sew;
a time to keep silence,
and a time to speak;
a time to love,
and a time to hate;
a time for war,
and a time for peace.
—Ecclesiastes 3:1-8

LET US PRAY

Dear Creator God, we worship you with our praise and thanksgiving. We praise you for your creation. We thank you for setting up this world with its times and seasons. Amen.

Alex • protector • Greek

33

READ
Isaiah 11:6-9

The cow and the bear shall graze together.
—Isaiah 11:7

Convert great quarrels into small ones, and small ones into nothing.
—Chinese proverb

Wildlife Peace

One day at a wildlife sanctuary, a hungry, stray kitten wandered into the pen of a 600-pound grizzly bear as he ate from a bucket of food. The bear, Griz, had grown up at the wildlife sanctuary, because his mother died when he was very young.

When the caretaker saw the kitten get close to the bear, he was worried. Certainly the bear would swipe the kitten with its huge paw and maybe kill it.

The kitten mewed when it saw the food. Griz looked up and tossed some food to the orange ball of fur. The hungry kitten pounced on the food and started to eat.

Soon the kitten, whom the caretaker called Cat, came regularly to eat with Griz. Cat preferred to live with the bear rather than with humans. Cat would rub against the bear, bat him on the nose, and play with him like cats do. Cat would even sleep right under the bear's jaws because it knew that was a safe place. Griz sometimes carried Cat in its slobbery mouth. The two became best friends and lived together a long time.

Our verses in Isaiah 11 (see also Isaiah 65:25) give us a picture of a beautiful kingdom of peace that we can expect in heaven. Like the garden of Eden, all creation will live in peace with no pain, no hate, no war, and no fighting.

The story of the bear and the kitten teaches us that we can live the kingdom of peace right now. We don't have to wait for some time in the future. Jesus taught us to speak peacefully to each other, to love our enemies, and to befriend people that others don't like.

The account of the bear and cat is a true story from Wildlife Images Rehabilitation and Education Center in Oregon. Both the bear and the cat have died, but statues have been erected in their memory.

What would the world be like if everyone got along?

What could you do today to help others live at peace?

We are children of peace;
our hearts overflow with peace;
our mouths speak peace;
and we walk in the way of peace.
—Menno Simons (adapted)

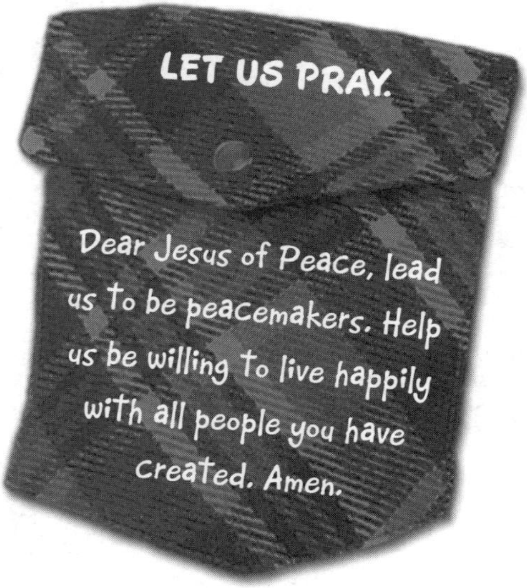
LET US PRAY.
Dear Jesus of Peace, lead us to be peacemakers. Help us be willing to live happily with all people you have created. Amen.

34

God-Comfort

READ
Isaiah 25:8-9

God will wipe away every tear from their eyes.
—Revelation 7:17b

"I don't get it," said Hana. "If heaven is such a great place to be, why do people always cry at funerals?" She and her family were returning from the funeral of an elderly neighbor who had been ill for a long time.

"It's hard for us to understand heaven," her mother said, giving Hana a hug. "As Christians, we believe that heaven is a wonderful place where God has a big party waiting for us."

"So, then, why do we cry at funerals?" Hana repeated.

Why do we cry—at funerals or any other time?

We're not like babies who cry a couple hours a day to tell us they need something. When we cry, it's often because we feel some kind of pain or hurt that doesn't go away. Maybe we miss someone who has died or moved away.

Our eyes begin to water; warm tears roll down our cheeks. Our faces scrunch up, and we begin to sob. Sometimes it's hard to stop. We usually feel better only when someone offers a hug or some other kind of help.

The Bible promises that God will wipe away our tears. Imagine God with a great big box of tissues that people on earth can use to comfort those who are hurting.

We look forward to a time in heaven when there will be no more crying. Until then, we can count on God, the great Comforter, to help us get through tough times.

Quien bien te quiere te hara llorar. (Whoever really loves you will make you cry.)
—Spanish proverb

When have you cried recently?

How has a friend helped you through a sad time?

Crying

When I'm sad and when I cry,
Count my tears until they dry.
Hold me, Comforter above.
Wipe my face with all your love.

When I'm hurting and in pain,
Soothe me, hold me once again.
Bandage up my broken soul,
Jesus, Healer, make me whole.
—J.G.K.

LET US PRAY

Thank you, Jesus, for helping us when we are sad. Thank you for people who comfort us when we are hurting. Amen.

Hana • blossom • Japanese

35

READ
Isaiah 40:28-31

Have you not known? Have you not heard? The LORD is the everlasting God, the Creator of the ends of the earth. He does not faint or grow weary; his understanding is unsearchable.
—Isaiah 40:28

God with Us Prayer

When we wake,
When we rest,
God of all,
Be our Guest.
—J.G.K.

God Present

In the van on his way home from the soccer game, Dylan was tired. He wanted to stay awake and talk with his friends, but he couldn't. He leaned his head against the window and closed his eyes.

As he dozed off, he could hear voices but couldn't understand them. His head was heavy. His jaw hung open. When his water bottle fell from his hand and hit the floor, he jerked. He opened his eyes to discover the other guys looking at him.

"Are you with us?" one of them asked.

All of us need sleep and rest. With the right amount, our body is fresh and strong again. Without enough sleep, we get cranky and we can't think straight.

Even though sleep and rest are part of our lives, God never needs to sleep. Another name for God is Yahweh, which means "the One who is always present." Even adults get tired and have to sleep. But God doesn't. God is always concerned about us, always rested, and always with us.

How much sleep do you need?

In what ways do you notice that God is always with you?

Omnipresence—All of God is present everywhere at once.

Can You Count the Stars?*

Can you count the stars that brightly
Twinkle in the midnight sky?
Can you count the clouds, so lightly
O'er the meadows floating by?

God, the Lord, doth mark their number
With His eyes that never slumber;
He hath made them ev'ry one,
He hath made them ev'ry one.
—Wilhelm Hey (H. W. Dulcken translation)

LET US PRAY

Great and loving God,
we praise you because you
care for us every day of
our lives. Thank you for
being with us and for
never sleeping.
Amen.

How much sleep do we need each night?

Newborns	16-19 hours
3-month old	13-15 hours
6-12 months	12-14 hours
Ages 1-4	10-12 hours
Ages 5-12	10 hours
Teens	9 hours
Adults	7-8 hours

Dylan • born from the ocean • Welsh

36

READ
Isaiah 55:8-9

My thoughts are not your thoughts, nor are your ways my ways, says the LORD.
—Isaiah 55:8

God T-shirt

Ryan grabbed a T-shirt from the laundry basket of clean clothes. He slipped it over his head and it hung on his body like a sack.

"Hey, this isn't mine. It's way too big," Ryan said to his older brother. "It's Dad's," he said, taking it off and searching for one his own size.

T-shirts come in many different sizes. There are children's sizes and adult sizes in small, medium, large, extra-large, extra-extra large, and even extra-extra-extra large.

If God wore T-shirts, what size would God wear?

Sometimes we think that God must be like humans because we are humans and we want God to be like us. But no matter how hard we might try, we will never be able to find a T-shirt that is God's size. God doesn't act like we act. God's thoughts are not our thoughts. God's acts and thoughts are enormous compared to ours.

If God were human, what color T-shirt would God wear? Probably one with many colors, since God loves all people. And if God is like that, we can try to love everyone, too.

Would God's T-shirt fade? Would God's T-shirt shrink or stretch out? Probably not, since God's T-shirt is perfect all the time.

Now imagine a T-shirt that covers the whole earth and all of the sun and stars. Even that would be too small to describe God's ways and thoughts.

God is a great eye. He sees everything in the world.
—Arabic proverb

How big is God?

What might God think about that you don't ever think about?

Who is God?

The Bible describes God in many ways.
Here are some of them:

Author
Creator
Eternal
Father
Forgiving
Friend
Glory
Good
Guide
Help
Holy
Immortal
Infinite
Judge
Just
Law-giver
Life-giver
Listener
Loving
Merciful
Nurse
One
Rescuer
Rock
Savior
Spirit
Truth
Unchangeable
Wise
Word

LET US PRAY

We praise you, God in heaven, for your ways and your thoughts. They are far greater than anything we can understand. Thank you for caring for your creation. Amen.

Ryan • young royalty • Celtic/Gaelic

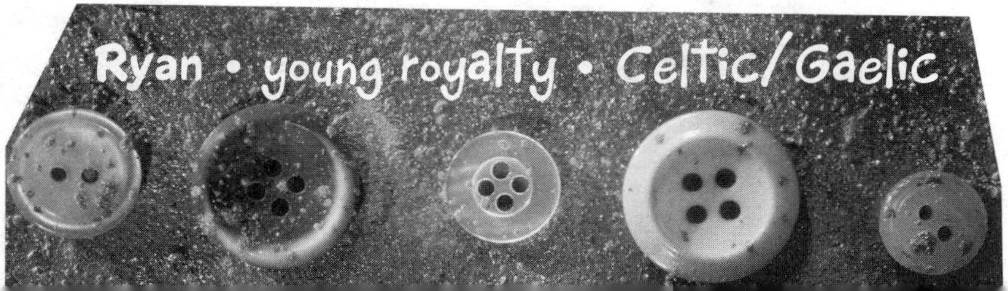

37

Decisions, Decisions

READ

Daniel 1:1, 3-6, 8 (or tell the story from Daniel 1)

To you, O God of my ancestors, I give thanks and praise, for you have given me wisdom and power.
—Daniel 2:23

It wasn't the new school or the new house or even the new city that bothered Olivia. It was the new neighborhood. She missed her old friends and favorite play places. Now Olivia was trying to figure out how to fit in.

A kid down the block had offered her a cigarette, and Olivia knew that was wrong. Other times, when she was with some of the new kids and her parents weren't around, she didn't always know what was okay to do and what wasn't.

In today's story Daniel was faced with decisions. He and other Jewish young men had been forced to move to a new city called Babylon. It was a long way from their home in Jerusalem.

Now they were told to eat foods that Jews didn't eat. Did Daniel eat the foods the Babylonians gave him? No, he decided to follow what he had been taught and to honor God.

Like Daniel, we too make decisions every day about how to care for our bodies, or how to act. Some decisions are hard to make. Some are easy. Whatever we do, our decisions help other people know what we think about God.

What good decisions have you made recently?
(Cheer and clap for each one named.)

What decisions might you make today?

Daniel

(Read this poem responsively. The leader reads a line, and worshippers respond with the same words. Clap once for each accented syllable, four times for each line.)

Daniel, Daniel sure is wise.
Daniel, Daniel wins the prize.

"Give me veggies, please," he says,
"Rich foods seem to rot my head."

This he tells the palace boss,
Who is serving up the sauce.

Ten days straight Dan eats his beets;
Ten days straight he gives up meats.

Does our Daniel prove his cause?
Sure he does—with God's applause.
—J.G.K.

LET US PRAY

Dear God, sometimes we wonder if we are making the right choices. Help us to honor you and others in the decisions we make each day. In Jesus' name we pray. Amen.

Olivia • peace (of the olive tree) • Latin

38

Flood Waters

At the dinner table, Grandpa Art told about a time when his sheep were stranded in the middle of the pasture. The flood waters were rising around them. The sheep heard Grandpa's calls but were afraid to swim to safety.

"I knew I had to do something," Grandpa said as everyone listened intently. "I swam across the creek. I wrapped my arm around the neck of one of the biggest sheep and pulled it into the water and across to the other side. Then the rest followed. I even remember that a couple of the lambs were riding on their mothers' backs. All of the sheep made it across safely.

"The next day when I went back, that place in the pasture was all flooded." Like all good shepherds, Grandpa knew the sheep, and he knew how to take care of them.

In the book of Micah (5:2-4a), we read a poem that was written long before Jesus was born. The poem describes a kind shepherd who gently leads us to find God's love and peace.

When we look at Jesus, we recognize him as just that kind of shepherd. Jesus' way of leading was different from the way mean leaders tried to rule others through fear. With Jesus as our shepherd, we have nothing to fear. Micah 5 tells us that God's Good Shepherd leads us in the way of peace.

READ
Micah 5:2, 4–5a

He shall be the one of peace.
—Micah 5:5

When have you needed someone to guide you?

Tell about someone who cares for you like a shepherd.

LET US PRAY.

Dear Jesus, thank you for caring for us in the same way a shepherd cares for sheep. Thank you for feeding us, protecting us, and guiding us today and every day. Amen.

Savior, Like a Shepherd Lead Us*

Savior, like a shepherd lead us,
much we need thy tender care.
In thy pleasant pastures feed us,
for our use thy folds prepare.
Blessed Jesus! Blessed Jesus,
thou hast bought us, thine we are.
Blessed Jesus! Blessed Jesus,
thou hast bought us, thine we are.

We are thine, do thou befriend us,
be the guardian of our way.
Keep thy flock, from sin defend us,
seek us when we go astray.
Blessed Jesus! Blessed Jesus,
hear, O hear us, when we pray.
Blessed Jesus! Blessed Jesus,
hear, O hear us, when we pray.
—anonymous

Art (Arthur) • noble strength • Celtic/Gaelic

39

Mountain Climbing

READ
Habakkuk 3:17–19

God, the LORD, is my strength; he makes my feet like the feet of a deer.
—Habakkuk 3:19

"I can't take another step," Dexter complained on his first hike in the mountains. "My feet keep slipping. My backpack is too heavy. I'm almost out of breath. I have to stop right now."

Dexter plunked down on a rock and let the other hikers pass him. "If this is what mountains are like, I don't ever want to see another one!" he said.

A song in the book of Habakkuk tells us that God gives us feet like the feet of deer on a mountain. Have you ever watched mountain animals? Their feet are made for running quickly and easily, even on steep slopes.

Many people struggle when they climb mountains. Getting to the top is hard work! We sometimes describe our problems as mountains. Even when we keep working on the troubles, they may not go away.

The next time you have a problem, pretend you are a deer who runs joyfully on the mountainside. When we run with God, we can get over even the highest mountains.

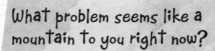

What problem seems like a mountain to you right now?

How is God helping you work on your problem?

LET US PRAY

Dear Lord, you are my strength. You are the one I turn to when my life seems like an uphill climb. Thank you for helping me solve the problems I face. Amen.

Run with Me

Run with me, Lord, to the heights of your love
Drive all my doubts and worries away.
Strengthen me now with feet like the deer
Run with me, Lord, on the mountain up here.

Run with me, Lord, wherever I go,
From the mountains above to the valleys below.
I will rejoice though the path seems so steep
Run with me, Lord. Up the mountain we'll leap.

—J.G.K.

Dexter • able-bodied • Latin

40

READ
Zechariah 9:9-10

[The LORD] makes wars cease to the end of the earth.
—Psalm 46:9

World Peace

"What's wrong?" Lucy asked her mother. "Is someone hurting those children?"

The magazine pictures seemed to be talking to Lucy. They told stories of war and sadness. They showed children who lived together in an orphanage because their parents had died. The children didn't have enough food, clean clothes, or warm beds. They looked sad.

Lucy's mother looked at the pictures. "Hate. That's what's wrong," she said. "People think fighting with people they hate will make the world a better place to live. Often, when there is war, parents die and children are left by themselves."

Today's Bible reading is from a song that describes a time when all the world will live in peace. The word pictures show a king getting rid of weapons used in war. The king is bringing "peace to all nations" (Zechariah 9:10).

Jesus rode into Jerusalem not on a horse of war, but on a donkey of peace. Jesus taught the way of peace. How sad it is that even today, many people still think they have to fight to solve their problems.

During today's worship time, let's imagine a whole day without fear. Imagine a whole day without fighting words. Imagine a whole day without violence of any kind. Maybe that day is today, and maybe peace will start with you!

We Pray for Peace

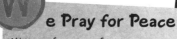

We pray for peace, for peace among the nations.
We pray for peace, goodwill among the people.
'Til love comes down like a summer rain;
'Til the rivers of justice flow again,
'Til the day of jubilee is come.
We pray for peace upon our planet home.
—Ken Medema

Q

What would it take for people in our world to stop fighting?

What might God want us to do to bring peace?

LET US PRAY

God of Peace, fill us with love. Help us to stop the hate and the fighting. Help us to live at peace with everyone around us. Amen.

The Volume of Friendship*

Lord, make a factory of peace,
Make more hope,
Hate, the least.
Make war as small as a speck of sand
And terrorism a wick on a candle that burns to ashes.
And make love and peace as big as a skyscraper.
And hope like a mountain that's 1,000 feet tall.
And make the volume of friendship be so loud
It shakes the ground.
—Alex House

(Sojourners magazine, April 5, 2005; written when the author was eight years old.)

41

READ
Matthew 1:18-21

An angel of the Lord appeared to [Joseph] in a dream.
—Matthew 1:20

Secret Messages

Chloe and her friend Grace loved to go to the city playground, because that's where they could tell secrets to each other. While other children played on the slides, the two girls would stand far apart from each other and whisper into metal cones that were connected by a long pipe.

Chloe and Grace chatted back and forth. They didn't care so much about what they said. They just liked the way these cones let them talk to each other at a distance. Even though they only whispered, they could hear each other perfectly.

Most of us like to get secret messages. They make us feel special because we are the ones chosen to get important news.

In the first chapter of Matthew, we read that an angel took a secret message to Joseph, telling him not to be afraid. God's big news for Joseph was that Mary's baby was God's Son and that Joseph was to name him Jesus. Joseph believed the angel and obeyed God's message.

God's secret about the baby Jesus is wonderful news for us. This is one secret that we can share with others. We too can be like angels of good news when we tell others about Jesus.

What good news do you have to share?

Has an angel ever spoken to you?

LET US PRAY

Thank you, God, for letting us in on the secret about Jesus. This is good news that we want to share. Amen.

I've Got a Secret

I've got a secret, a secret in my heart,
I've got Jesus, yes, Jesus in my heart,
I've got love, yes, love is in my heart,
I've got the good news of Jesus in my heart.

I'm gonna tell the world the secret in my heart,
I'm gonna tell the world of Jesus in my heart,
I've got love and peace, yes, they are in my heart,
I'm gonna tell the world of Jesus in my heart.
—J.G.K.

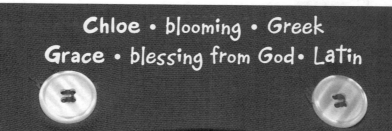

Chloe • blooming • Greek
Grace • blessing from God • Latin

42

Worship Cheers

READ
Matthew 2:10-11

On coming to the house, the wise men saw the child with his mother Mary, and they bowed down and worshiped him. —Matthew 2:11 International Children's Bible

"Praise God! Praise God! Praise God!" the children called. It was worship time at summer Bible school, and today everyone was cheering.

"Is God great?" asked the teacher.

"Yes," they responded.

"Is God awesome?"

"Yes, yes!" they cheered.

"Is God creator?"

"Yes, yes, yes!" they yelled. "Praise God! Praise God! Praise God!"

In the Bible, people of Israel worshipped God in many ways when they came together. They gave thanks and praised God. They sang and they prayed. They encouraged each other with words of faith. They stood and kneeled and sat. They gave offerings of money and other possessions. They used their talents to honor God.

Just as the wise men from the East worshipped the child Jesus, we too worship Jesus, our God and Savior. How do we worship? We pray, we sing, we read from the Bible; we repeat words that praise and honor our God. We give our money and use our talents to honor God. We obey God each day of the week.

We worship God—sometimes alone, and sometimes with others—because God has called us as God's faithful children here on earth. Praise God! Praise God! Praise God!

What parts of worship are most meaningful to you?

In what new ways would you like to worship God at home?

O Come, All Ye Faithful*

O come, all ye faithful, joyful and triumphant,
O come ye, O come ye to Bethlehem.
Come and behold him, born the king of angels.
O come, let us adore him,
O come let us adore him,
O come let us adore him,
Christ the Lord.
—John F. Wade

LET US PRAY

Dear Jesus, like the wisemen we honor you today with our love and devotion. Help us to know how to love and serve you faithfully. Amen.

Great, great, great

The Hebrew language has no comparing words like **better** and **best** or **smaller** and **smallest**. During worship in Jesus' time, when people wanted to call God the "greatest," they would repeat the word **great** three times: "great, great, great." The prophet Isaiah once heard some angels call out, "Holy, Holy, Holy is the Lord." They meant, "God is holiest of all" (Isaiah 6:3).

43

Big Mystery

Larisa had to read her report on potatoes to her class. "The Mystery of the Potato," she began. "The potato hid in South America for centuries until people found it was good to eat. When explorers from Europe arrived, they discovered the potato and took it back with them to Europe. At first, people in Europe thought it was poisonous. Then they realized how good it tasted. They planted more and more potatoes. The potato traveled all over Europe, then to North America and all around the world. It surprised people wherever it went."

The child Jesus traveled a lot too. He moved with his family from Bethlehem in Judea to the land of Egypt. Then they settled in Nazareth, in Galilee.

For the people who lived when he did, his life was a mystery. King Herod and others didn't understand that Jesus was God's Son here on earth. They thought he was someone to be feared. But Mary and Joseph knew Jesus was someone special, someone sent by God to share the Good News in a way people on earth could understand.

There are many things we don't understand. We sometimes call them mysteries. Each day, as we learn, we understand more and more. We can trust God to help us understand each mystery at just the right time.

Today let us be especially thankful for Jesus, who helps us uncover the mystery of what God is like. As we learn more about Jesus, we also learn more about God.

READ
Matthew 2:13-14, 19-23

Joseph got up, took the child and his mother, and went to the land of Israel.
—Matthew 2:21

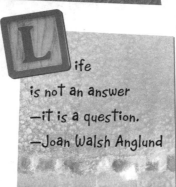

Life is not an answer—it is a question.
—Joan Walsh Anglund

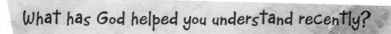

What has God helped you understand recently?

What things about Jesus are hard for you to understand?

In the Bulb There Is a Flower*

—Natalie Sleeth

In the bulb there is a flower;
in the seed, an apple tree;
in cocoons, a hidden promise:
butterflies will soon be free!
In the cold and snow of winter
there's a spring that waits to be,
unrevealed until its season,
something God alone can see.

LET US PRAY.

We worship you, Almighty God,
because you help us
understand things that seem
like mysteries to us here on
earth. Thank you for Jesus,
our Savior and Lord. Amen.

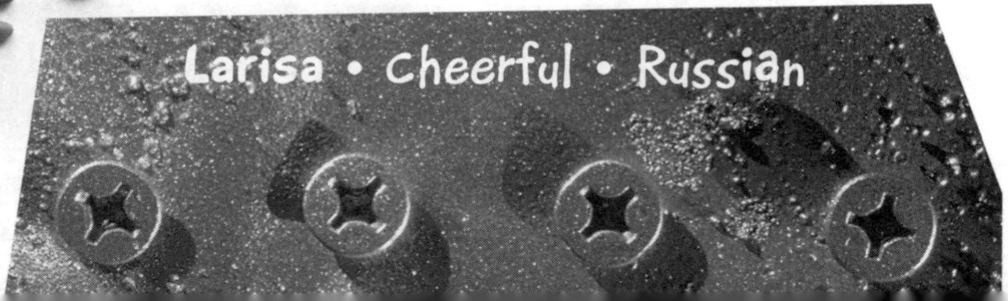

44

READ
Matthew 3:13-17

A voice from heaven said, "This is my Son, the Beloved, with whom I am well pleased."
—Matthew 3:17

Connect the Dots

Caleb liked connect-the-dot pictures. He would begin with a page that was blank except for numbers and dots. Beginning with the number one dot, he would draw a straight line to number two and then to three—until he'd connected all the dots. Then he could see the whole picture. Sometimes many, many lines made one picture.

Our lives are like a book of connect-the-dot pictures. We move along from one activity or event to another. Bit by bit, as we follow Jesus, we understand more about God's plan for us.

Early during his time here on earth, Jesus showed that he accepted God's special purpose for him. Through his baptism, Jesus showed that he wanted to connect all the "dots" of God's plan to bring people back to God.

We too can "connect the dots" of our lives. We can choose God's way as our own path. When we commit ourselves to God, we feel God's love just as Jesus did when he was baptized.

What kinds of puzzles are your favorite?

What does it mean to commit ourselves to God?

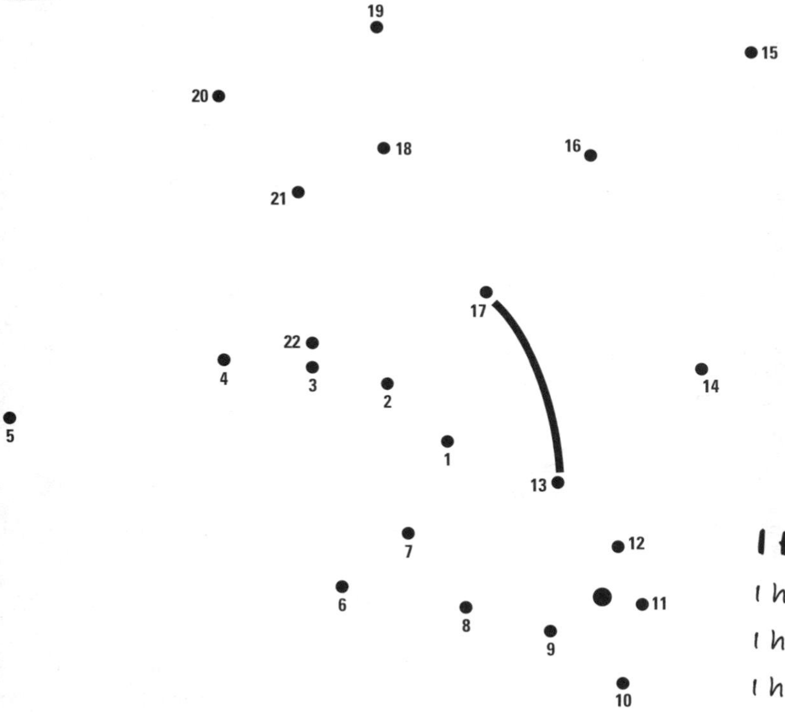

LET US PRAY

(Read a line, and have the others repeat it.)
Help us, Jesus, to trust you.
Help us, Jesus, to follow your example.
Help us, Jesus, to obey you always.
Amen.

I Have Decided to Follow Jesus*

I have decided to follow Jesus,
I have decided to follow Jesus,
I have decided to follow Jesus,
No turning back, no turning back.

—Traditional

Caleb • faithful • Hebrew

45

Jesus' Heartbeats

READ
Matthew
4:18-22

He said to them,
"Follow me."
—Matthew 4:19a

At his physical exam in the doctor's office, Clay was fascinated with the stethoscope. The doctor let him listen to his own heart beat. Then he gave Clay a hollow rubber ball filled with water.

"Squeeze it like this," the doctor said, squirting Clay with a spurt of water. "When you squeeze the ball, some of the water comes out. After each spurt, you relax your grip and the ball comes back to its round shape again. This is the way the heart works."

When the heart squeezes blood throughout the body, the heart helps the body do its work. The heart does not work alone. Veins and arteries move the blood where it needs to go.

To do his work on earth, Jesus chose people. The first ones he selected were his disciples, who went where he went and learned from him. They watched all he did and listened to what he said. He asked them questions about what they were learning and explained to them what they had seen. He taught them important lessons from God.

Just as the heart sends the blood throughout the body, so Jesus sends us to serve others. You and I have important talents that we can use to help Jesus as we do his good work.

As you feel your heartbeat, remember Jesus who is calling and sending you.

Imagine you are one part of the human body that is helping Jesus. Which part would you be? (Example: I would be an ear because I like to help people by listening as they share their problems.)

What is Jesus calling you to do today?

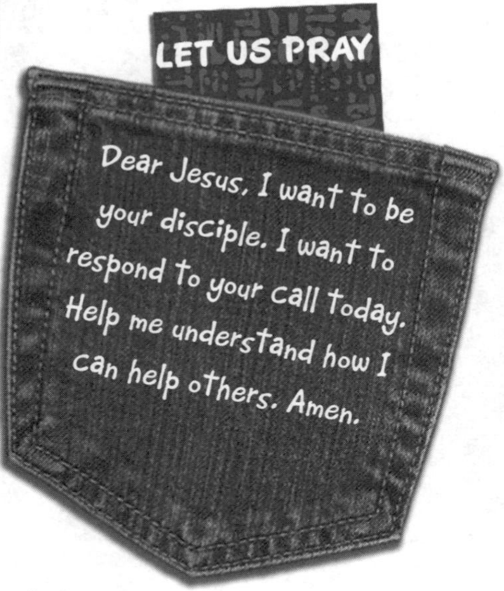

Disciples-In-Training*

We are disciples in training,
we're learning from the master,
we're on the road with Jesus,
wherever he may lead.

We are disciples in training,
we're part of the adventure,
we're on this road together,
let's see where it will lead.
—Bryan Moyer Suderman

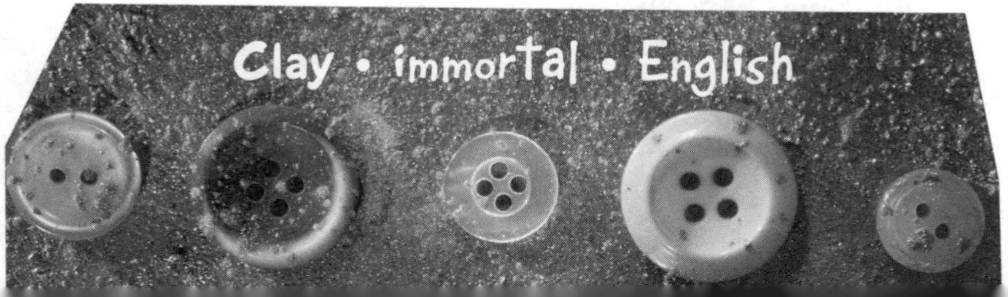

46

READ
Matthew 4:23-25

Jesus went throughout Galilee teaching, . . . preaching . . . and healing.
—Matthew 4:23
New International Version

Jesus' Garden

Bianca liked to water the marigolds. She had helped plant the yellow flowers in the community garden near her home. She knew it was important to take care of them.

She filled the watering can at the faucet and lugged the water to the other side of the garden. Sometimes the water splashed on her clothes and shoes.

"This is hard work," she said to one of the other children. "It would be easier if all the plants would come to where the water is!"

Jesus knew the importance of going to the people. He took the good news of God's kingdom to the people. He preached to them. He healed them. Like a gardener taking care of a garden, Jesus took care of people everywhere.

We, too, can water the flowers in Jesus' garden, by being kind to all people. Jesus wants us to find people where they are. We can go to visit older people who can't leave their houses. We can walk over to a neighbor who needs a friend. Our smiles and encouragement can help others grow. When we share God's love with others, it's like carrying water to thirsty plants in a garden.

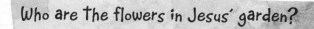

Who are the flowers in Jesus' garden?

How can you carry Jesus to people today?

Make me a flower,
a smile by the street,
planting your beauty
in people I meet.
Make me a flower
that's sent here and there,
wishing your kindness
on all who need care.
—J.G.K.

LET US PRAY

Dear Jesus, you are the gardener who plants us and takes care of us. Lead us to help others who need your care today. Amen.

Love stretches the heart and makes you big inside.
—Margaret Walker

Bianca • fair-skinned • Latin

47

READ
Matthew 5:1-11

Blessed are the meek.
—Matthew 5:5

The blessing is not in living, but in knowing how to live. —Mexican-American proverb

Upside Down

Madilyn was practicing her clarinet. "What song are you learning?" Madilyn's mother called from the other room. "It doesn't sound like any you have been playing."

Madilyn knew the notes sounded funny. She called back, "I've got the book turned upside down, and I'm trying to figure out if I can recognize the songs without looking at the titles."

Do you like to look at the world upside-down? It sure changes your view!

Often, the Bible changes our view of the world.

The verses we just read from Matthew are called the Beatitudes. They help us understand what it means to be truly happy. But Jesus' ideas of happiness are upside-down, compared to how most people think of happiness.

Jesus teaches us that instead of needing to be in charge, we are happiest when we are gentle and polite. Instead of boasting about how great we are, Jesus wants us to serve others.

Jesus' teachings help us question what the world thinks is important. They help us look at ourselves to make sure that the things we think are important are also the things which are important to God.

When have you been truly happy?

How would you change or improve the world?

LET US PRAY

O Jesus, we want to understand your "upside down" words. Help us look at ourselves in new ways, so that we can become more like you. Amen.

The Beatitudes

Blessed are the poor in spirit,
for theirs is the kingdom of heaven.
Blessed are those who mourn,
for they will be comforted.
Blessed are the meek,
for they will inherit the earth.
Blessed are those
who hunger and thirst for righteousness,
for they will be filled.
Blessed are the merciful,
for they will receive mercy.
Blessed are the pure in heart,
for they will see God.
Blessed are the peacemakers,
for they will be called children of God.
Blessed are those
who are persecuted for righteousness' sake,
for theirs is the kingdom of heaven.
Blessed are you
when people revile you and persecute you
and utter all kinds of evil
against you falsely on my account.
Rejoice and be glad, for your reward is great in heaven.
—Matthew 5:3-12

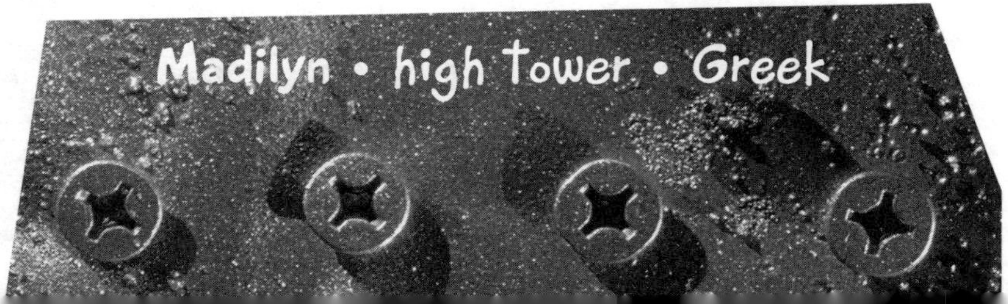

48

Salty People

READ
Matthew 5:13-16

You are the salt of the earth.
—Matthew 5:13

Rachelle and her family spent a Saturday morning in the kitchen, making salt dough ornaments. They mixed salt, flour, water, and food coloring to make stars and animals to give to children in the hospital. Rachelle's favorites were the pink lion and the red lamb.

"Why do we use so much salt?" she asked as she poured a cupful into the next batch of dough.

"Because that's what the recipe says," her older brother responded.

Jesus knew that people need salt in order to live. Our bodies need a certain amount of salt to be healthy. We use salt to flavor and to preserve foods like cheese, pickles, and meat. We use salt to melt snow and ice. We use salt to make soaps, dyes, paint, paper, rubber, batteries, cosmetics, fire extinguishers, and many other things we use.

When Jesus tells us to be the salt of the earth, he means more than the salt shaker on the table. He wants us to take God's flavor into all parts of our lives. He wants us to season the entire world with love, peace, patience, and kindness.

Let's go now, and be salt in the world!

How does your family use salt?

How are you like the salt of the earth?

You Are Salt for the Earth*

You are salt for the earth, O people,
salt for the kingdom of God!
Share the flavor of life, O people:
life in the kingdom of God!

Bring forth the kingdom of mercy,
bring forth the kingdom of peace.
Bring forth the kingdom of justice,
bring forth the city of God!

—Marty Haugen

Rachelle • lamb • French

Salt Dough Ornaments

- 2 cups flour
- 1 cup salt
- 1 cup water
- Food coloring (optional)
- Holiday cookie cutters
- Decorations, glitter, paint

Combine flour and salt in a large bowl and mix well. Mix water and food coloring. Add a little liquid at a time to the flour mixture. Knead 7-10 minutes. Store in a plastic bag in the refrigerator. Roll dough ¼ inch thick and cut out shapes with cookie cutters. Bake at 325-350°F/160-180C on foil-covered baking sheet. Paint and decorate as desired.

LET US PRAY.

Dear Lord, you have taught us to be the salt of the earth. Help us share your love as we sprinkle kindness on people we meet today. Amen.

49

Rain Down

READ
Matthew 5:43-48

Love your enemies.
—Matthew 5:44

The sun glowed warm and bright on two boys as they waited for the library to open. Standing far apart, they glared at each other. Whenever they could, they would say mean things to each other.

As they waited, the sky darkened, and heavy rain splattered on them. Soon both boys ran to the one small, dry space near the door. The rain seemed to be playing with them, blowing first one way and then the other, so that the boys had to move together to stay dry.

When the library door finally opened, the two boys ran in, laughing about the way the rain had brought them together.

The space we occupy on this earth is space that we share with others. But we humans are good at putting up walls everywhere so that we don't have to be friends with others, especially those who are mean. Sometimes the walls are real, and sometimes we just imagine them.

Individuals, families, groups, and countries fight about silly things. "No, you can't sit here," we sometimes say to others. "No, you can't eat here. You can't live here. Don't cross this line onto my land."

One of the most important things that Jesus did while he was on earth was to teach us how to love. Jesus calls us to love everyone, even people who don't like us. The word love in these verses is agape (or God love). Jesus tells us to share our space the way God would, showing kindness toward all.

Have you ever drawn a line to keep someone out?

How does God want us to act when people are mean to us?

Rain Down*

Rain down, rain down,
Rain down your love on your people.
Rain down, rain down,
rain down your love, God of life.

God of creation, we long for your truth,
You are the water of life that we thirst.
Grant that your love and your peace touch our hearts,
All of our hope lies in you.

—Jaime Cortez, based on Psalm 33

LET US PRAY

Dear God, erase the lines that keep us apart from others. Forgive us for hurting others. Encourage us to share our space because you are the God of love. Amen.

Game: Your Shoes*

Imagine you are someone else in the family. Pretend to put on that person's shoes and become him or her. How does it feel to walk in his or her shoes and to experience life like this person does?

Take turns asking each other questions about what it's like to be the other person. Sample questions:

- How does it feel to be the parent?
- How does it feel to have a hearing aid or glasses?
- How does it feel to be the oldest, middle, youngest, or only child?

50

READ
Matthew 6:9-13

Lord, teach us to pray.
—Luke 11:1

If praying is talking with God, and it is, then surely any one that can talk can pray.
—Samuel K. Landis*

Prayer Suitcase

Andy's dad lifted the last suitcase into the van. It was finally summer vacation, and everyone in the family was eager to leave on their trip.

"Before we go, let's have a traveling prayer," Andy's dad said. The family stood in a circle and held hands.

"Let's say the Lord's Prayer," Andy offered. "We don't have to remember to pack it because we already know it by heart."

When Jesus taught his disciples to pray, he gave them the Lord's Prayer as a model. This short prayer is like a prayer suitcase. It's packed with what we need to pray to God.

The Lord's Prayer teaches us to think of God as a loving Parent who is very important to us. It teaches us to ask God for help in living as we depend on God. It teaches us to ask God for forgiveness and for strength to keep from doing wrong.

This prayer connects us not only with God, but also with people. Christians everywhere know the Lord's Prayer. When we say it in our homes and churches—or carry it with us on a trip—we are holding hands not only with God, but also with others around the world.

What would a picture of the Lord's Prayer look like? (Draw pictures.)

How does the Lord's Prayer make you feel?

Our Father in heaven,
hallowed be your name.
Your kingdom come.
Your will be done
on earth as it is in heaven.
Give us this day our daily bread,
and forgive us our debts
as we also have forgiven our debtors.
And do not bring us to the time of trial,
but rescue us from the evil one.
For the kingdom
and the power
and the glory are yours forever. Amen

LET US PRAY

Thank you, God, for prayer that connects us to you. We pray now as Jesus taught us. (Recite the Lord's Prayer together; use the version that is most familiar to your family.)

Why do Christians pray "Our Father"?

In the Lord's Prayer (Matthew 6:9-13 and Luke 11:2-4), Jesus calls God "Father." In Aramaic, the language Jesus spoke, the word for father was Abba. That was what Jewish children called their fathers. It really meant Daddy and showed love and closeness between the dad and his children. That's how Jesus experienced God! Because Jesus prayed to God this way, the early church also used the word Father when praying to God.

Andy (Andrew) • strong • Greek

51

Good Orchard

READ
Matthew 7:15-20

Lead lives worthy of the Lord, fully pleasing to him, as you bear fruit in every good work and as you grow in the knowledge of God.
—Colossians 1:10

Johann and his family spent a morning picking oranges in the orchard. Johann liked to be the first one up the ladder to pick because he could find the biggest oranges and fill up his baskets before anyone else. He was always amazed how many oranges one tree produced and how every tree was just a bit different from others.

Imagine you are like a tree. Your roots draw their water from God. As your roots grow bigger and bigger, you understand better who God is, who you are, and what you believe.

As a tree's branches spread in all directions, you too are moving here and there as you learn to know God's people and world. Like an orange tree, you are "bearing" fruit. Whenever you do a good deed, you are bearing fruit for the Lord.

When you see a tree today, take time to say a prayer as you remember your connection to God.

If you were a tree, what kind would you be? Why?

In what ways are good Christians like trees?

LET US PRAY

We want to be strong trees for you, dear Lord. Teach us how we can be more like you in all we do and say. Amen.

Trees Puzzle

Many trees are mentioned in the Bible. Use your Bible to match each tree and Scripture verse. (Answers are on page 209).

1	almond	a	Genesis 6:14
2	cedar	b	Exodus 15:27
3	cypress	c	Deuteronomy 6:11
4	fir	d	Psalm 104:16
5	mustard	e	Psalm 104:17
6	oak	f	Isaiah 1:30
7	olive	g	Jeremiah 1:11
8	palm	h	Ezekiel 17:5
9	sycamore	i	Matthew 13:31-32
10	willow	j	Luke 19:4

Johann • God is gracious • German

52

Sand Castles

READ
Matthew 7:24-27

Everyone then who hears these words of mine and acts on them will be like a wise man who built his house on rock.
—Matthew 7:24

The campers spent the last afternoon of summer camp on the beach, building sand castles. With waves gently lapping at their feet, they carried shovels, buckets, plastic silverware, and tin cans in search of a good place to build. Those who had never built sand castles asked others to help them.

"The trick is to find the right spot," Michael explained to his group. "If you go too close to the water's edge, the waves will come in and destroy the buildings. If you stay too far away from the water, the sand will be too dry and we'll have to carry too much water."

First they dug a hole to find the water below the sand. Then they pulled wet sand out of the hole and piled it up.

"A good foundation is very important," Michael said, showing the kids how to create sand bricks. The sand castle grew higher and higher until, an hour later, the group stood up to admire their work. Even though a few waves had pounded their creation, it stayed standing.

When Jesus told the story we read today, he knew that any building needs a good foundation. In the story, the wise builder constructs a house on rock. The foolish one builds a house on sand. When the winds and rains come, the house that remains is the one with the solid foundation.

Jesus is the foundation of our lives. Each of us has times in our lives when bad thoughts or feelings try to push us away from Jesus. When we keep connected to Jesus and to other followers of his, we are much stronger than we are without him.

When have you needed a good foundation for something you made?

How does Jesus want our churches to be strong?

Rock or Sand

Imagine you're a tiny house.
You don't know where to stand.
You don't know where to put your feet—
on rock or on the sand?

It might be fun at first to slide
your toes into the land
and wander here and there throughout
the silly, shifting sand.

But Jesus says that wise ones build
on rock that's rather grand.
God is our Rock. Stand firm with him.
Forget about the sand.

—J.G.K.

LET US PRAY

Dear Jesus, as we walk with you each day, keep us close to you, our Rock. Amen.

Michael • Who is like God? • Hebrew

53

Running Errands

READ Matthew 10:1-4, 7-10

[The twelve] departed and went through the villages, bringing the good news and curing diseases everywhere.
—Luke 9:6

Mom's directions were clear: "Buy stamps at the post office. Put stamps on the birthday invitations. Drop the invitations in the mailbox. Be home in 30 minutes." Paige and Shawana liked running errands for their mother. Going to the post office or the store was fun. It made them feel important.

When we run errands or do jobs around the house, we do so to help others. Even if we don't always know how to do the job at first, we can learn from someone else. A good teacher gives good directions and makes us feel that we can do the work.

Jesus chose the twelve disciples because he knew they could do his work. He gave them clear directions. Go out, he said. Do the work. Heal people. Tell them the good news about God's kingdom.

Jesus has chosen us, too. Whoever we are and wherever we live, Jesus calls us. Sometimes we hear his call through other people. Sometimes Jesus calls us to do his work right away. Sometimes, he puts an idea into our heads and we do the work later. If he gives us work to do, we know that he trusts us to be able to do it.

What jobs do you like to do for others?

When have you felt like Jesus' disciple?

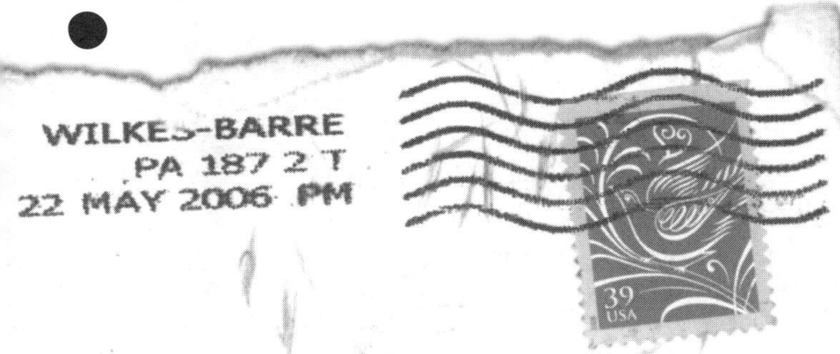

How wonderful it is that nobody need wait a single moment before starting to improve the world.
—Anne Frank

LET US PRAY.

We are willing, dear Jesus, to run errands for you. Lead us so that we too can learn to share the good news about God. Amen.

Disciple Questions

For each question below, choose the correct answer. For help, see the lists of the 12 disciples in Matthew 10:1-4, Mark 3:13-19, and Luke 6:13-16. Answers are on page 209.

1. The word disciple means . . .

a. one who believes in Jesus; b. a student of a teacher; c. one of the 12 whom Jesus called; d. all of these.

2. Which of these was not one of the 12 disciples?

a. Philip; b. Bartholomew; c. Judas Iscariot; d. Paul.

3. The disciples did many things as they followed Jesus. Which one did they not do?

a. listened to and learned from Jesus; b. traveled with Jesus; c. healed people; d. wrote the book of Psalms.

4. Which one of these disciples was not a fisherman?

a. Andrew; b. James; c. John; d. Matthew.

5. Three disciples were best friends of Jesus. Which one was not (see Matthew 17:1)?

a. Thaddeus; b. James; c. John; d. Peter.

Paige • assistant • French

Shawana • grace • Swahili

54

Family Tree

READ
Matthew 12:46-50

Whoever does the will of my Father in heaven is my brother and sister and mother.
—Matthew 12:50

At the dinner table George talked about his science project on plant families.

"What are plant families?" asked his sister Holly.

"Well," he replied, "there are so many different plants in this world that someone decided to group them together to make it easier to study them. Each group of plants is called a family because of the way they are alike."

"Are they grouped by color?" Holly asked.

"No," said George. "It's the kind of plant they are. All the cactus are together, and all the maple trees are together, and all the sunflowers are together. Each plant belongs to a family."

"Do they all live together in families like we do?" Holly asked.

The family laughed as they thought of funny things plants would do if they were like humans. They imagined the grasses sitting at the dinner table. The pines would play games together. The carrot family would meet for family gatherings.

We use the word *family* in many ways. The word usually means a group of related people like parents, children, and other relatives. Can you think of other ways we used the word family? *(Wait for responses, like family doctor or family name.)*

We sometimes call the church the family of God. Jesus taught us to love and accept others as we do our own families. That's why sometimes we use the words *sister* and *brother* to describe others we know who love Jesus. Christians everywhere make up the branches of God's family tree. Whenever we are together, it's like we're at a family gathering!

What is your favorite part of being in a family?

Why does Jesus want all of us to be together like a family?

LET US PRAY

Dear God, you have put us together in families. Help us to love others as we love our own families. Amen.

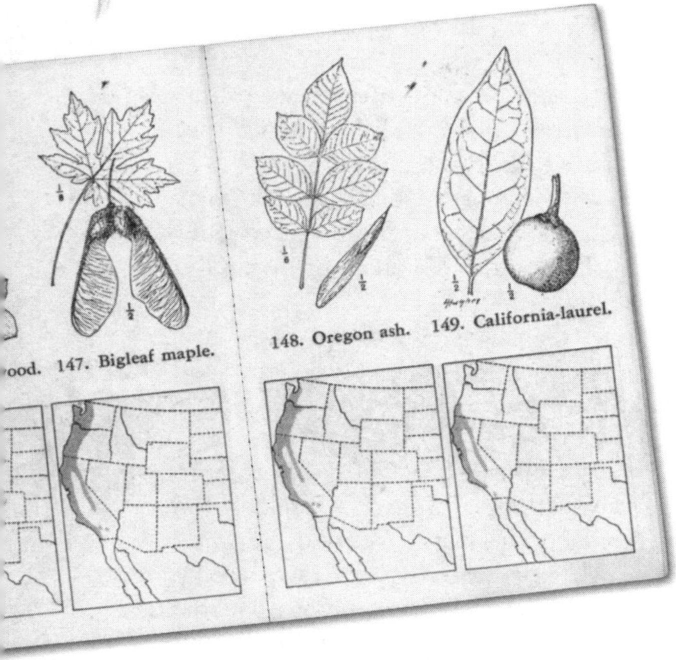

God's Family song*

God has a fam'ly with many people:
Grownups and children who love God today.
We get together to care for each other
to worship and learn how to follow God's way.
All grownups, all children,
all mothers, all fathers
are sisters and brothers in the fam'ly of God.

—Patricia Shelly

George • farmer • Greek

Holly • plant with red berries • English

55

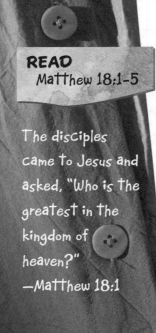

READ
Matthew 18:1-5

The disciples came to Jesus and asked, "Who is the greatest in the kingdom of heaven?"
—Matthew 18:1

Kingdom Play

The new coach saw the problem right away. All the players wanted to have the ball at the same time.

"You're hogging the ball," the coach told them at halftime. "Pass it off before the players on the other team get to you. Dribble only a little or not at all. Then pass it to someone who is not surrounded by players from the other team. You'll be better players if you think of the team and not just yourself."

Has anyone ever told you that you were hogging the ball or wanting to be the center of attention? At some time or another, all of us do things we think will make us more important than others.

In Matthew 18 we hear the disciples ask Jesus, "Who is the greatest in the kingdom of heaven?" This was their way of asking, "Which of us does God think is most important?"

Jesus surprises the disciples with his answer. "Become like a child," Jesus says, "and then you will know God." Was it possible for grown-up men to act like children again?

"Change your thinking," Jesus says. Being really great on earth is not important in God's kingdom. Some of us like to brag a lot or show off. Some of us wear stylish clothes or buy the best of everything only to draw attention to ourselves. Some of us want to hog the ball or be the center of attention all the time.

Jesus' way is different. Jesus wants us to change our attitude and think of others first.

Why do people like to brag?

How does Jesus want you to act if you are on God's team?

God's Team

We want to be on God's team.
We want to change our ways.
We want to reach the kingdom goal
And learn the kingdom plays.
—J.G.K.

LET US PRAY

Dear Jesus, you are far greater than we will ever be. We need your help as we change our thinking and attitudes. Help us learn to think of others first. We want to be on your team. Amen.

56

READ
Matthew 20:1-16

The kingdom of heaven is like a landowner who went out early in the morning to hire laborers for his vineyard.
—Matthew 20:1

God often pays debts without money.
—Irish proverb

What's Fair?

Isabella stomped up the stairs in disgust.

"We worked a lot longer and harder than Evan did. You can't treat him the same as the rest of us," Isabella complained. Their mother had promised a reward for cleaning the basement. Now, instead of paying money, she wanted to take them all out for ice cream.

"That's not right," Isabella yelled. "He sat around while we did all the work. Is that what you call fair?"

Often we find ourselves caring only about what is fair for us, not about what is fair for everyone. When we think this way, we are thinking like humans. But God's ways are different. God's standards are based on love, not on our selfish ideas of fairness.

Jesus calls us to think differently about our questions. Instead of "How much do I get?" or "Is that fair?" Jesus wants us to ask, "How much can I give?" or "How much can I serve?"

Getting lots of money can be a very selfish goal in life. We need money to live, but the first thing Jesus asks us to think about is what we can do to serve others and treat them fairly.

What would you tell Isabella?

The next time you think about saying, "That's not fair!" what might you say instead?

Fairness Poster: What does fairness look like?

Talk about ways you try to be fair. On a large piece of paper, draw a picture to show what it means to be fair. Or cut out words and letters from magazines and put together sentences that describe peace and justice for all people.

LET US PRAY

Dear Jesus, as we study your stories about how to live, help us to understand what you want to teach us. Today we want to do what's right and fair. In your peace and love, we pray. Amen.

Evan • God is gracious • Welsh

Isabella • Consecrated to God • Italian

57

READ
Matthew 20:29-34

Lord, let our eyes be opened.
—Matthew 20:33

Crying Baby

Alyssa's baby sister cried all the time. Grandma said she had colic. The only time Kimmie was quiet was when Grandma held her and walked around and sang to her.

"Are we going to have to take Kimmie to the doctor?" Alyssa asked.

"Perhaps," said Grandma, "but for now I'm praying that God will heal Kimmie and help us know how to take care of her."

Think of a time when you were hurting, when you needed someone to hold you close. All of us know what it's like to feel pain or to be around someone who is hurting.

Jesus knew how to heal. He knew how to place his hands on those who were hurting and make them well. Today we read how two men asked him for sight. He touched their eyes, and they could see.

When we are hurting, we too can call to Jesus and ask him to help us. Jesus wants only what is good for us. Even when we have to wait for healing, we know we can trust Jesus to care for us.

Close your eyes now and feel Jesus holding you. Let him touch your hurts.

Tell about times when God answered your prayers for healing.

When has Jesus opened your eyes to see the hurts of others?

Heal Me

Come and heal me, Lord, today.
Drive the pain and hurt away.
Touch me now and let me see
As I pray on bended knee.

In my worries, heal me, Lord.
Help me not to feel ignored.
Lift me up and hold me tight.
Come, be with me through the night.

Heal me now of this disease.
Take away my cough and sneeze.
I just want to feel okay.
Touch me now, O Lord, I pray. Amen.
—J.G.K.

LET US PRAY

Lord, open our eyes and help us see. We pray for healing for people we know who are hurting (insert names). Grant us your kindness and love, and be with us whether we are sick or well. Amen.

Alyssa • rational • Greek

Kimmie (Kimberly) • ruler • English

58

READ
Matthew 21:1-11

Look, your king is coming to you, humble, and mounted on a donkey.
—Matthew 21:5

Hosanna

The word *hosanna* was first used in Hebrew prayers to invite God to the time of worship (Psalm 118:25). It meant "save us now." In Matthew 21 and when we use it today, it also means "praise God."

Peace Message

Anthony pedaled his bike down the hill. He often used this hilly stretch after delivering the last newspaper on his route. As he rode faster, he felt his jacket stick to his body as the force of the air pushed it back against him. He stuck out his arms to see how long he could ride without putting his hands on the handlebars.

"Wheeeee! Here I come," he yelled as he passed joggers and walkers. They smiled as they watched him speed down the hill.

Like Anthony and his newspapers, Jesus had a message for the world: God's good news of peace for all people.

Jesus entered Jerusalem on a humble donkey, not on the tall horse that an army general would have ridden. Still, he got the attention of the people in the city, bringing joy to them. The people waved branches from palm trees (John 12:13) and shouted, "Hosanna! Hosanna!" The people believed Jesus was someone special who was coming in God's name. He was greater than any king they'd seen.

In our day, on Palm Sunday, we celebrate Jesus' entry into Jerusalem. Like the people in Jerusalem, we might wave palm branches to tell others that Jesus is our special leader.

We still honor Jesus and his message of peace. Today we cheer, "Hosanna. Hosanna in the highest heaven! Jesus is Lord and King."

When we say, "Hosanna," it means we honor Jesus above all else. How do you honor Jesus?

How could you deliver God's message of peace to someone you know?

HOSANNA

Hosanna poem

As Jesus comes to us in peace,
Our hands we stretch and raise.
Hosanna to God's very Son.
We sing. We dance. We praise.

So shout with us to God's own Son.
His greatness we proclaim.
Our King now comes, bless'd is our Lord.
Hosanna to his name!
—J.G.K.

LET US PRAY.

Dear Jesus, we invite you to come to us today with the message of peace. Enter our homes as we honor you. Hosanna. Hosanna. We bow to you. Amen.

Anthony • worthy of praise • Greek

59

Waiting and Waiting

READ
Matthew 25:1-4

The kingdom of heaven will be like this. Ten bridesmaids took their lamps and went to meet the bridegroom.
—Matthew 25:1

It seemed to Kayla that she spent her whole life waiting. She waited for the school bus; she waited for Grandpa. She waited for programs to start; she waited for classmates to line up. She waited for dinner. She waited for Christmas. She waited for summer.

Had she been waiting all her life? Kayla wondered.

We spend our lives waiting. Sometimes waiting is hard work. Sometimes we think we are ready for something to happen but right at the last minute, we forget. Sometimes we wait so long that we aren't ready when the time comes.

Jesus told the parable of the ten bridesmaids. It's a story about helpers at a wedding. Some were ready and had extra lamp oil to put in their lamps when their lamps ran out. Some weren't ready and had to go back for oil. Then they were so late for the wedding they were not allowed in. Jesus told this story to remind people to be ready when he comes again.

Like these wedding helpers, all of us make choices and decide for ourselves what is important. Sometimes we are wise. Sometimes we are foolish. Fortunately, God's Spirit is ready all the time to help us make good choices and to help us even when we seem foolish.

Who or what do you often wait for?

What important decisions have you made or would you like to make so that you are ready for God?

LET US PRAY

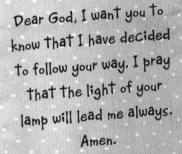

Dear God, I want you to know that I have decided to follow your way. I pray that the light of your lamp will lead me always. Amen.

Olive Oil

People in Bible times used olive oil in many ways.

FOR LIGHT

Lamps burned oil made from olives. The flame would be at the end of a flax wick in a shallow clay bowl.

FOR THE HOME

Olive oil was important for cooking, baking, soapmaking, perfumes, medicine, and lotion.

FOR CEREMONIES

When people wanted to dedicate someone or something to God, they often anointed the person or thing with oil.

FOR A SYMBOL

Oil was so important during Bible times that it became a symbol of joy and love.

FOR JESUS

Messiah and Christ, words that we often use to refer to Jesus, mean "the anointed one."

Kayla • Crown of laurels • Hebrew

60

READ
Matthew 25:34-40

I was hungry and you gave me food, I was thirsty and you gave me something to drink, I was a stranger and you welcomed me.
—Matthew 25:35

Laundry Game

Sandra was up to her neck in laundry. Since her grandma wasn't supposed to walk steps and the washer was down a flight of stairs, Sandra was doing all the laundry by herself. She'd already finished four loads and had more to do.

"I'm trying to keep Grandma from walking steps," she told her neighbor, "so I've invented what I call 'The Great Laundry Game.' For each load, I give myself points for every item of clothing I fold and put away. Then I compare the scores of all the loads. If the work feels like a game, it's more fun."

We like to play games and have fun. We also can have fun helping others.

These verses from Matthew 25 describe the kingdom of God. This kingdom is a world where God is in charge. That world can be found in our own everyday lives on earth and in heaven in the future.

Imagine that the kingdom of God is like a game. Imagine that we get points every time we help someone. Imagine that we get the most points for helping those who badly need help. Throughout life we have many opportunities to improve our score.

Sometimes we don't even realize how much we are helping others. But God knows and remembers. Each time we help someone, we do God's work. Each day we live, we live for God.

What is your favorite game to play with others?

In what ways can you make helping others fun?

The time is always right to do right.
—Martin Luther King Jr.

LET US PRAY

Dear God, since we are your children, everything we do is important to you. Help us play the game of life in a way that will bring honor to you now and always. Amen.

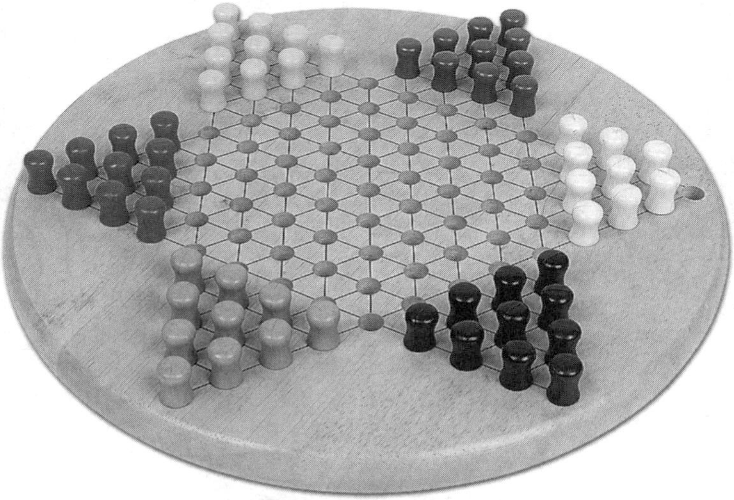

Sandra • helper of humanity • Greek

61

READ
Matthew 26:26-29

Do this to remember me.
—Luke 22:19
International Children's Bible

Plant Names

"Why do our houseplants have names?" Brinda asked. "Other people don't name their plants."

Her mom had the answer. "The first plant I named was a peace lily I got from a friend when my granny died, so I named it Granny. Then I got the prayer plant that is in our terrarium and named it after Grandpa. Then I decided to name all my plants after special friends and family members. The plants help me remember people I've been close to, and I like that."

Do you ever forget things? Everyone does. Jesus knew that sometimes we humans forget what is really important. When he shared his last meal with the disciples, he served them bread and drink and said, "Do this to remember me."

Today, 2,000 years later, we still remember Jesus. The Lord's Supper, often called communion, is a special time of worship in all Christian churches. The bread and the drink remind us of Jesus, who lived with us here on earth, died on the cross, came back to life, and promised to live in our hearts forever.

What things do you give names to? Why?

What do you have in your home to remember Jesus?

LET US PRAY

Lord Jesus, we remember you. Thank you for living among us. Thank you for giving us the freedom to love and serve you now. Thank you for promising to live in our hearts forever. Amen.

I Will Remember

I will remember my Jesus, my Lord,
I will remember the words that he said,
I will remember the stories he told
and the message from God that he spread.

I will remember the peace that he preached,
I will remember the people he healed,
I will remember the kindness he showed
and the wonderful love he revealed.

—J.G.K.

62

Broken Mirror

READ
Matthew 26:69-75

Above all, love each other deeply, because love covers over a multitude of sins.
—1 Peter 4:8
New International Version

God forgives sinners, otherwise heaven would be empty.
—German proverb

"Yes, you did."

"No, I didn't."

"Yes, you did. I saw you go in there. Then I heard something break. I know you did it."

Ava wished she was a bird so she could fly away and not have to face her sister. Ava had broken her sister's favorite mirror. It fell off the counter when Ava walked by.

"I didn't break it. It broke by itself," Ava said, trying to offer an excuse.

"A mirror can't fly off the counter by itself. If you don't admit you broke it, your problem is going to get bigger."

Lying can get us into a heap of trouble. Even if we feel like running or flying away from the problem, it won't go away. Once we start to tell lies, it's hard to stop. Then others don't know when they can trust us. It can be hard to patch up a friendship when trust is broken.

In Matthew 26 we read about Peter, one of Jesus' good friends. At the time of Jesus' arrest, Peter told others he did not know Jesus. Three times Peter told that lie. How bad Peter felt later! He cried and cried. Saying he didn't know Jesus was like breaking the mirror that reflected everything he had done with his friend.

The good news for Peter and for us is that forgiveness has the power to mend broken friendships. It takes courage to say, "I'm sorry. Will you forgive me?" or "I forgive you." Admitting we're wrong can hurt a lot. But when someone forgives us, we feel good. We can go on to become what God wants us to be.

Have you ever lied to cover up a mistake?

Do you have any relationships that are broken? What can you do today to start to mend them?

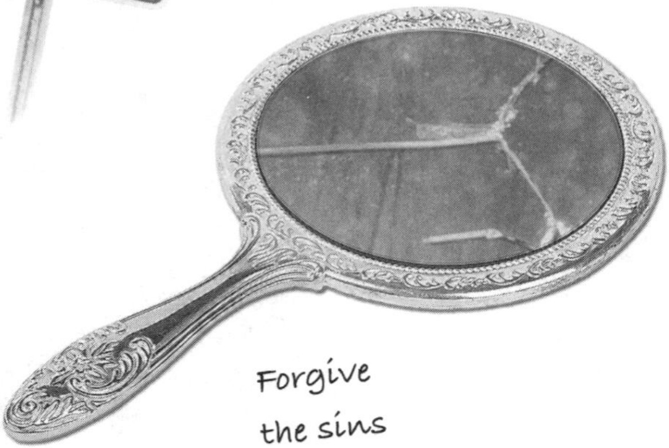

Forgive
the sins
we have done,
just as we
have forgiven
those
who did wrong
to us.

—Matthew 6:12
International Children's Bible

LET US PRAY

Dear Jesus, sometimes we tell lies because we're afraid of the truth. Forgive us, and help us learn to forgive others when they hurt us or tell lies. In your holy name, we pray. Amen.

Ava • like a bird • Latin

63

Best Story

READ
Matthew 28:1-10

"[Jesus] is not here; for he has been raised, as he said. Come, see the place where he lay." —Matthew 28:6

Imagine that you took all the stories in the world, put them together in one room, and had to choose the best one. Which one might you choose? *(Wait for response.)*

Every day we hear and read many stories. Some are pretend. Some are real. But there is no story more important than the real one that tells of Jesus' resurrection. On this we base our faith and believe in a living God.

How could the story of Jesus be complete, if he wasn't raised from the dead? Jesus' birth and good deeds were miraculous. Jesus healed and changed people. Jesus even died on the cross for us.

But the greatest story of all tells of Jesus' power over death. When we believe that Jesus rose from the dead and follow him as our living Lord, we are changed forever.

It is this Jesus whom we worship. It is this Jesus who lives in our hearts. Now, let's go tell the world!

What are your favorite stories about Jesus? How do they help you understand God?

What questions do you have about Jesus' resurrection?

Glory chant

(Listeners chant the words "Glory. Hallelujah" in rhythm after you read each line.)

Here's a story of our Lord.
  Glory. Hallelujah.
Born a babe in Bethlehem.
  Glory. Hallelujah.
Came from heav'n to live on earth.
  Glory. Hallelujah.
Called us all to follow him.
  Glory. Hallelujah.
Taught us how to love and live.
  Glory. Hallelujah.
Healed the sick and served the weak.
  Glory. Hallelujah.
Journeyed to Jerusalem.
  Glory. Hallelujah.
Died for us and lives again.
  Glory. Hallelujah.
Lives in heaven evermore.
  Glory. Hallelujah.
Light for all the world to see.
  Glory. Hallelujah.
  GLORY. HALLELUJAH!
  GLORY. HALLELUJAH!

LET US PRAY.

O risen Lord, we believe in you. We worship you. We celebrate you. Help us tell the world about you. Come into our hearts and live in us forever. Amen.

day will come after night,
summer will come after winter,
warm days will come after cold days;
and always food will grow after seed is sown. This is a promise."
Then God said, "Look up at the sky, Noah. I have put
18
a sign there to help everyone remember what I have promised."
Noah looked up. He saw a beautiful rainbow in the sky!
And even today, when we see a rainbow, we remember that God keeps His promise, and that He takes

64

Amazing Gifts

READ
Luke 1:5–14

You will have joy and gladness.
—Luke 1:14

Gifts reflect those who give them.
—Chinese proverb

Ted rubbed his eyes, still tired after a night's sleep. He wondered what was in the brown box on the breakfast table. It wasn't his birthday or Christmas or any other special day he could think of. He wasn't even sure it was for him, but there it was, right at his place.

His stepmom read his mind. "It's yours, Ted," she said. "It may look like an ordinary box, but inside is a special gift from me for you."

Sometimes we don't know a real present when we see one. Sometimes what at first seems like an odd, boring present turns out to be one that we will treasure.

Zechariah was a priest who worked in the temple in Jerusalem. He and his wife, Elizabeth, were good people who talked to God often in prayer. They often told God they wished they had a baby.

One day in the temple Zechariah received a strange present. It wasn't a wrapped package that he could see. Instead, Zechariah received the gift of good news, delivered by an angel.

"Your prayer has been heard," the angel told Zechariah. "Elizabeth will have a baby."

But Zechariah couldn't believe it. "How can this be?" he asked. "We're too old to have a baby!"

Sometimes answers to our prayers surprise us. We may even question God's answers. But it is true that God gives us some amazing gifts. Living close to God gives us special joy.

Think about a time when you got a wrapped package that you didn't expect. How did you respond?

What amazing gifts has God given you?

Child Blessing

You will have joy and gladness,
You will have peace and good will,
You will have love sent from our God above,
the gift of good news come to earth.

You will have words for speaking,
You will have wisdom to serve,
You will have blessings from our God above
who raised up a Savior for us.
—J.G.K.

LET US PRAY

Dear God, help me to be willing to accept all gifts you offer to me. Thank you for good people whose lives have helped me know you better. In your name I pray. Amen.

Ted (Theodore) • divine gift • English

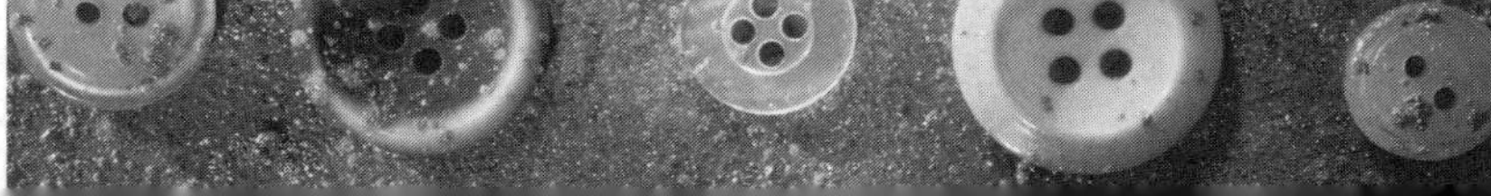

65

READ
Luke 1:26-33, 37-38

Mary said, "Here am I, the servant of the Lord." —Luke 1:38

Crumb Manager

"Why do we always have to clean off the table and no one else does?" Derek asked his dad after their family had eaten in the fast-food restaurant.

"You can thank your great-grandpa for that," Derek's dad responded. "I remember that whenever Grandpa ate with us and was done eating, he would hold his plate against the edge of the table and wipe all the crumbs onto the plate. It was just a little thing for him to do, but he did it every time he ate."

"And that's why you called him a crumb manager?" Derek asked.

"Yes," said Dad. "We learned that habit from him, and now you are, too."

People remember acts of service like cleaning crumbs off a table. Simple things like pushing in your chair, making your bed, hanging up your towel, or putting away your toys can help those who live with you. Being a servant to others and helping them do their work are signs that we are servants of God.

When an angel visited Mary with a special message, Mary called herself a "servant of the Lord." Her willingness to serve God by becoming the mother of Jesus is the reason that people remember her today.

We too are called to be servants today. When we feel nudged to wipe crumbs off the table or to do some other kind deed, that is God calling us to service.

What was it about Mary that made her the right person to be the mother of Jesus?

What good deeds does God want you to do today?

LET US PRAY

Dear Jesus, nudge us to do kind deeds of service for others each day. We thank you for people who have taught us simple acts of service. Amen.

Mary

"Greetings, dear Mary,
the Lord is with you.
God wants to bless you
in all that you do."

Mary, surprised by
this heavenly one,
questioned the visit
and what she had done.

"Don't be afraid now
'cause God's pleased with you.
Listen now, Mary,
this message is new.

"You'll have a baby—"
This isn't pretend.
You'll name him Jesus.
His kingdom won't end."

"I am your servant,"
was Mary's reply.
"I am your servant,
O, Lord God Most High."

Lord, we're your servants,
You're with us today..
We are your servants,
We'll follow your way.

—J.G.K.

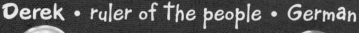

Derek • ruler of the people • German

66

Candlelight

READ
Luke 1:76-79

The people who walked in darkness have seen a great light. —Isaiah 9:2a

"Why does the wax disappear when a candle burns?" Frankie asked. During dinner he had watched the first candle in the family's advent wreath burn down. Now, he was puzzled. Where did the wax go?

Do you know the answer to Frankie's question? *(Wait for responses.)*

When we light a candle, heat from the flame melts the wax. The melted wax turns into an invisible gas that becomes the candle's fuel. The candle burns because of the wax that gives it the power to burn.

For thousands of years candles have provided light for people in the dark. Today we have other sources of light too, but we still use candles for special occasions. Candles often remind us of Jesus, the light of the world.

In this Scripture from Luke 1, we have a picture of Jesus helping people understand God's power and truth. Even though many years have passed since Jesus came to earth, his light continues. Because of the power in his flame, we walk in God's light and in the way of peace.

As you watch a candle burn, think of Jesus and his power to give you energy and light to live for him. Then you can share his light and love with those around you.

Turn your face to the sun and the shadows fall behind you. —Maori proverb

When have candles helped you?

What does the light of Jesus help you see?

LET US PRAY

Dear Jesus, you are the light of the world. Bless us now with understanding. Help us see new ways to spread your light to others. Amen.

Jesus Is Light

Jesus has come. He is the light.
We sit in darkness no more.
See in the light—beauty and truth.
See now the peace we adore.

Right here, right now, Jesus shines bright.
Right here his glory we see.
Candles glow white, glimmer and shine,
Reflecting God's majesty.
—J.G.K.

Frankie (Frank) • free • Latin

67

Finding God

READ
Luke 2:1-20

This will be a sign for you: you will find a child wrapped in bands of cloth and lying in a manger.
—Luke 2:12

Amber's dad could find anything. He could find her eyeglasses. He could find her shoes. He could find her jacket. He could even help her find her smile. Each time he would find something for her, he'd remark, "I've saved the day. Now we can live again."

We often rely on family members or friends to help us locate lost items. Sometimes people find things for us before we realize they are missing.

The story of Jesus' birth is a story about finding God. For many years people had waited for the promised Messiah, the Son of God who would come to earth as our Savior.

Finally, in the fields outside Bethlehem, the angels told the shepherds how to find Jesus. They searched for Jesus, and when they found him, they told others about their amazing experience. Who would have thought to look for the Messiah in a manager in Bethlehem?

Finding Jesus and following him as our Lord and Savior is what it means to be a Christian. Today people are still finding Jesus through the story of his birth. When we find Jesus, we discover what is missing in our hearts. Then we can trust God to lead us always.

For what things do you often search?

Where have you found God?

LET US PRAY

Jesus, our Lord and Savior, we praise you as the angels did. We honor you as Mary and Joseph did. We thank you for finding us and giving us new life. Amen.

Now I've Found Jesus

Now I've found Jesus,
Like the shepherds and wise men.
Now I've found Jesus
In the light of his birth.

Now I've found Jesus
Our God and our Savior.
Now I've found Jesus
'Cause he's come to earth.
—J.G.K.

Amber • precious jewel • Arabic

68

Big Questions

READ
Luke 2:41-51

After three days [Jesus' parents] found him in the temple, sitting among the teachers, listening to them and asking them questions.
—Luke 2:46

"Why are you making that big question mark?" Ky asked Tanya. "It's as big as you are!"

"It's for my writing class," Tanya said. "First, I make this question mark, see? Then on it I'm supposed to write complete sentences that have question marks at the end."

"Do they have to be BIG questions since you're putting them on the BIG question mark?" Ky asked, laughing at his own question.

Some of us ask a lot of questions. Do you know anyone like this? *(Wait for responses.)*

Questions are important because they help us learn. They help us understand ourselves and our world. Questions help us solve problems and make decisions. They lead us to invent new things, improving life for ourselves and others.

Jesus taught us that it's good to ask questions. When he was twelve, he sat with the temple leaders and they patiently answered his questions. Later, as a teacher, Jesus often used questions to help people understand important things about God.

Questions about God are big questions, and we need to keep asking them. How do your questions help you understand God? Can you imagine a BIG question mark stretching all the way from you to heaven?

What big questions do you think Jesus was asking in the temple?

What big questions do you have for Jesus today?

The Question Game

Two or more players decide on a topic. One person starts with an open-ended question about the topic; then another responds with a related question. Players continue without making a statement or repeating a question.

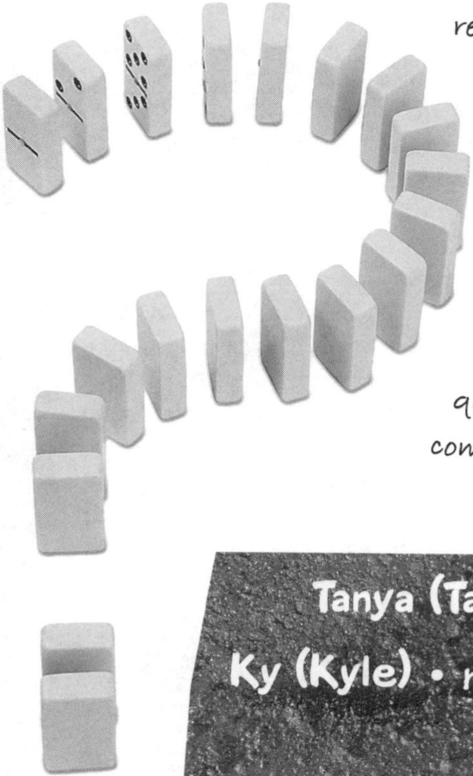

If the topic is God, players might ask these questions to start: Who is God? Where did God come from? How does God help people?

LET US PRAY.

Who are you, God? How can you be such a great and wonderful God and still care for me? What can I do to help you today? Amen.

Tanya (Tatiana) • queen • Slavic

Ky (Kyle) • narrow land • Celtic/Gaelic

69

READ
Luke 4:16-22

The Spirit of the Lord is in me. This is because God chose me to tell the Good News to the poor. God sent me to tell the prisoners of sin that they are free, and to tell the blind that they can see again. God sent me to free those who have been treated unfairly.
—Luke 4:18
International Children's Bible

Sand Play

Zofia and her friends sat in the sand pile, pretending the pile of sand was as big as the world.

"Pretend this is the moon," Zofia said, pointing to one corner of the pile. "And here is a big, tall mountain, and here is a desert. Over there is the North Pole."

They made smooth roads so their toy cars could drive from the desert to the North Pole. Then they sloshed water on the sand to make it stick together so they could make ice cream cones and caramel cake. The sand stuck to their skin as if it was glue, and they began to feel like sand people.

When we play, we imagine the world to be different. We may live on the moon or the North Pole. We can make castles, roads, ice cream cones—anything we can imagine. We can even become sand people.

Jesus changes us in ways we can hardly imagine. But Jesus isn't playing with us, and he is not pretending. He wants to help us be the people God wants us to be. That was why he came to earth. As his followers, we can help him make a world that shows his spirit of peace in everything.

Imagine the world as one big sand pile. Imagine that you have the hands to smooth out the rough places so that people can live in safety and freedom. With God's help, you can do it. With God's help, we can all do it.

What is your favorite kind of imaginary play?

How could you make the world a better place?

Do all the good you can,
By all the means you can,
In all the ways you can,
In all the places you can,
At all the times you can,
To all the people you can,
As long as ever you can.
—John Wesley

LET US PRAY

Dear Jesus, send us now to care for others as you have taught us to do. Let us love as you have loved. Let us serve as you have served. Amen.

Zofia • wisdom • Polish

70

READ
Luke 10:29-37

Who is my neighbor?
—Luke 10:29

Creed

Let me be a little kinder,
Let me be a little blinder
To the faults of those around me,
Let me praise a little more.
—Edgar Albert Guest

Elastic Meals

Rebecca and her family loved going to Grannie's to eat. Grannie wasn't Rebecca's grandmother, but like many grandmothers, she was always helping people.

Once, when Rebecca and her family had just sat down to Grannie's table for supper, the phone rang. Rebecca heard Grannie invite more people to join them.

"I always say that our meals must be elastic," Grannie told Rebecca as they set the table for more people. "They can stretch a long way." People like Grannie know how to reach out to others.

In the story of the Good Samaritan, Jesus teaches us to be like elastic—to stretch out as we care for strangers and people in need. Jesus wants us to move beyond what is easy.

Instead of offering only a band-aid, the Good Samaritan bandaged the man's wounds, took him to an inn, paid for his care, and promised to return with more money. His example reminds us to treat others as we would want to be treated—with kind words and actions. Jesus wants us to be like strong elastic, reaching out again and again to serve others.

Tell about a time when you saw someone be "elastic" in the way they treated others.

Who is your neighbor?

LET US PRAY

Thank you, Jesus, for the example of the Good Samaritan. Help us to show kindness as we stretch our love to neighbors near and far. Amen.

Healer of Our Every Ill*

Healer of our ev'ry ill,
Light of each tomorrow,
give us peace beyond our fear,
and hope beyond our sorrow.

Give us strength to love each other,
ev'ry sister,
ev'ry brother.
Spirit of all kindness,
be our guide.
—Marty Haugen

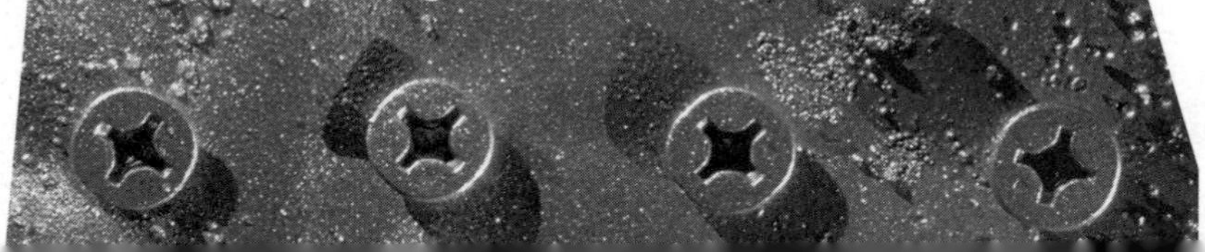

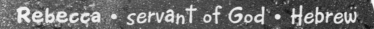

71

Subway Prayer

READ
Luke 11:5-8

Pray without ceasing.
—1 Thessalonians 5:17

Audrey stepped onto the subway with her aunt. Audrey dreaded the long ride. She grumbled to herself as she lugged her heavy backpack aboard and stumbled to a seat.

"What's wrong?" her aunt asked.

"I hate these long rides every day," Audrey complained. "What are people supposed to do while they ride? What do you do? You always seem so quiet and calm."

"I pray," her aunt said. "I pray for each person I see. I pray for people I don't see. I pray for people I know and those I don't. My mama taught me that. When she was riding the subway or in a taxi or bus, she'd be praying the whole time for people she didn't even know."

Pray all the time, Jesus tells us in the story about the midnight visitor. We can pray all the time—in the morning, at noon, in the afternoon, in the evening. We can even pray at midnight, and all the times in between.

Let's think of prayer as a long, long subway ride that lasts all day. When we hop on the prayer subway, God is with us. God visits with us as we sit together. God listens as we share our problems. God smiles as we talk about our happy times. God points out people we can help. Whether our trip is long or short, we can talk with God the whole time, and God will listen.

When is your favorite time of day to pray?

What words would you use to describe the way you pray?

Today before we pray, let's name people who need our prayers. Then let's name places (towns or countries) and pray for the people who live in those places. *(Wait for responses.)*

LET US PRAY

God, we lift up all these people to you. Today we are going to pray all the time as we ride the prayer subway with you. In Jesus' name we pray. Amen.

Prayer List

MOM, DAD
GRANDPA, GRANDMA
GRACE
AUNT RENA
UNCLE SETH
PEACE ON EARTH
MATH TEST
GEOGRAPHY
PATIENCE
BE KIND
PASTOR
SS TEAC

O Lord, Hear My Prayer*

O Lord, hear my prayer.
O Lord, hear my prayer.
When I call, answer me.
O Lord, hear my prayer.
O Lord, hear my prayer.
Come and listen to me.
—based on Psalm 102:1-2.

72

A Good Waiter

READ
Luke 11:9–10

Ask in faith, never doubting.
—James 1:6

In the restaurant Samantha stared at the confusing menu. She'd never seen one like it and didn't know how to tell the waiter what she wanted.

"May I take your order, please?" the waiter asked. Samantha was hungry, but she didn't know what she wanted to eat. Even after her family had suggested several items, the waiter was still waiting on her.

"Don't hurry," the waiter said. "I'll help you whenever you are ready."

Every restaurant is different, but waiters in all restaurants know it is their job to help. We can trust a good waiter to remember what we order and to supply us with everything we need to enjoy the meal.

What needs do you have today? Jesus encouraged his listeners to trust in God for all their needs. "Turn to God," he told them. "Pray to God," Jesus said, "and God will respond."

Let's think of prayer as a trip to a prayer restaurant. We go there because we are hungry to be with God and to know God. Like a good waiter, God longs to give us good gifts. God brings us what we need, stays close by—and even helps us when we spill the water.

What is your favorite place to eat?

What words do you use when you pray to God?

Hey, God,
I know you are there.
I hope you listen and respond.
You are a great God,
my loving parent,
my best friend.
Because of Jesus,
I can come to you with my needs.
Even when I cannot say the words,
I know your Spirit speaks for me.
I love you. I trust you. I depend on you.
May your blessings fill the earth
now and always.
In the name of Jesus, I pray.
Amen.
—J.G.K.

LET US PRAY

Before we pray, let's list the things we are worried about and the problems we face today. (*Wait for responses.*)

Thank you, dear Jesus, for teaching us how to pray. Forgive us for times when we have forgotten to bring our problems to you. We now ask for your help to live today for you. Amen.

Samantha • listener of God • Hebrew

73

Spider Worries

READ
Luke 12:27-29

Do not keep worrying.
—Luke 12:29

Melanie's family was at a rest stop on a long car trip. Before Melanie could get out of the van she made her granny promise to protect her from any spider she might see—especially the really big ones with long legs.

At the last restroom break, the big spiders in the sinks had scared Melanie so much, she'd spent the last two hours worrying about the next stop.

"I'll help you," Granny told her. "You don't have to worry about anything when you're with me."

Do you know anyone who worries all the time? Worries have a way of turning little thoughts into big problems. Big problems can keep us from enjoying life as God intended it to be.

Imagine those wild flowers we see along the highway. Jesus reminded us that flowers don't worry about how they look or how they will get water. Since we know that God cares for even the flowers, we can be sure that God cares for us.

As you worship today, give your worries to God. Trust God to take care of you. And the next time you see a flower, think of how much God cares for you.

What do you worry about?

How much time do you spend worrying?
What could you do with that time instead?

Worries

I can worry about spiders,
I can worry about bees.
I can worry about crickets,
I can worry about fleas.

I can worry in the nighttime,
I can worry in the day.
I can worry when I'm working
And when I am at play.

I can worry, worry, worry about most everything.
I can worry, worry, worry until my brain goes ding.
But God sets me free from my worry and distress,
And I know God cares for me, yes, yes, yes.
And I know God cares for me.
—J.G.K.

LET US PRAY.

Dear God, in you I put my trust. I ask you to take care of all my worries today. Amen.

Melanie • darkness • Greek

74

Dress Up

READ
Luke 14:7-11

Clothe yourselves with humility in your dealings with one another.
—1 Peter 5:5

Sarah and her sisters and friends spent Saturday afternoon playing dress up. They acted like royalty and had fun until the older kids tried to tell the little ones who they were supposed to be.

"How come they always get to be the ones in charge?" Katherine whispered to Sarah.

"They just think they're more important because they're older," Sarah told Katherine.

In real life some people give us the idea that they are more important than we are. They claim to know it all. They get the best places to sit, the best foods to eat, the best everything.

Jesus taught us not to think and act as if we're more important than others. He wants us to serve others and think the best of them. That's what it means to be humble. Jesus knew that when we think of ourselves as too important, we can have problems getting along with others.

When you let God be most important in all parts of your life, you will be a humble person. Like people dressing for the day, you will put on the "clothes" of humility.

Next time you get dressed, say a prayer as you put on each piece of clothing.

Tell stories about times when you dressed up or played a game in which you had to change how you looked.

How can thinking of others as important help you get along with them?

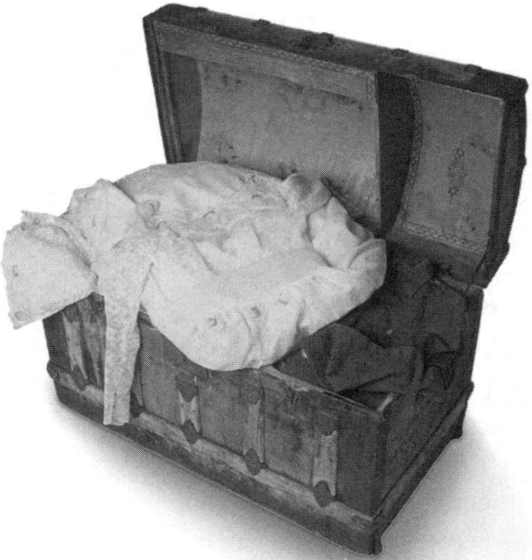

LET US PRAY

Dear God, we want to be like Jesus. We want to wear the clothes of humility in all we do and say. Amen.

Pure heart*

Give us
A pure heart
That we may see thee,
A humble heart that we may hear thee,
A heart of love that we may serve thee,
A heart of faith that we may live thee.
—Dag Hammarskjöld

Katherine • pure • Greek

Sarah • princess • Hebrew

75

READ
Luke 15:8-10

Rejoice with me, for I have found the coin that I had lost.
—Luke 15:9

Lights Out

In the late afternoon, Riley came home to discover that the electricity was off. She walked around the apartment, flipping light switches in each room, hoping that some light would turn on. After she called her mom at work, she phoned her neighbors.

"I'm alone, and it's getting dark. Can I come over?" Riley asked.

Over the phone line, she heard the little kids next door yelling, "Yea, Riley's coming over! Riley's coming over!"

When we are without light of any kind, it's good to know that people are nearby. We often feel lost and lonely when we can't turn on the lights, especially when it is dark outside.

Jesus told a story about a lost coin. It's a story that reminds us that Jesus is always looking for lost and lonely people—including us! When we are no longer lost, no longer separated from God's love, there's a great celebration. It's not only our friends and family on earth who share the joy; it's all the angels in heaven, too.

Look at the light around you and feel God close to you. Hear Jesus calling you. When you are no longer lost, and you say, "Yes," to him, be ready for the great celebration.

God is light and in him there is no darkness at all.
—1 John 1:5

When have you had a hard time finding your way in the dark?

When have you heard God calling you?

Lord Be Near Me

Lord, be near me when I'm afraid,
when I don't know what to say.
Lord, be near me when I'm alone;
when I cry, take me home.

Every time the clouds roll in
and every time the rain begins,
I pray to God to keep me safe
and hold me close for another day.

Lord, be near me.
—Joel David Krehbiel

LET US PRAY

Dear God, thank you for showing me your light of love and your way to Jesus. Thank you for seeking me and finding me. Today I want to say yes to you. Amen.

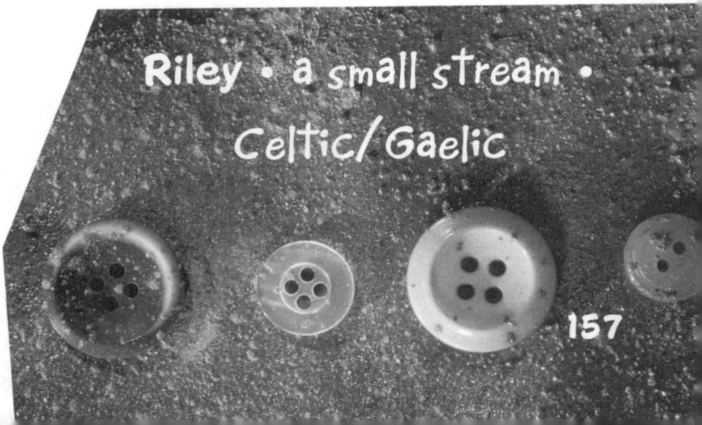

Riley • a small stream • Celtic/Gaelic

Ten Cents

READD

Luke 16:10-11

Whoever is faithful in a very little is faithful also in much.
—Luke 16:10

"Ten cents? You're going back to the clerk to return ten cents? We're already late and if you go back, we'll miss the first part of the game." Skyler couldn't believe that Dalton was making such a big deal over ten measly cents.

"I have to," Dalton said, heading back into the store to return the extra coin the clerk had given him in change.

Do you know people like Dalton who are extra careful about the little things? *(Wait for responses.)*

Jesus reminds us that we are responsible to take care of God's world. If God can trust us to take care of things that don't seem very important, then God can also trust us to take care of more important things.

We learn how to do big jobs by doing small jobs first. If we are honest with just a few cents, God knows we will be honest with bigger amounts of money. More and more, we show that we are responsible.

Why do you think Dalton returned the money?

What little things do you do each day to make life better in the world around you?

Little Drops of Water

Little drops of water,
Little grains of sand,
Make the mighty ocean
And the pleasant land.

Little deeds of kindness,
Little words of love,
Help to make earth happy,
Like the Heaven above.

—Julia Fletcher Carney

Little things are indeed little, but to be faithful in little things is a great thing.
—Mother Teresa

LET US PRAY

Thank you, Jesus, for reminding us to be responsible in our everyday lives. Please help us to be faithful in small things, so that we can learn to be faithful in big things. Amen.

Dalton • town near the valley • English

Skyler • scholar • Dutch

77

Garden Seeds

READ
Luke 18:15-16

Let the little children come to me.
—Luke 18:16

Leena and her dad had just planted big potatoes and onions in their garden. Now she helped with the little seeds. Her dad made a shallow trench in the soil. Leena poured beet seeds into her palm and carefully placed the seeds in the row.

"Why do we plant so many beets in our garden?" Leena asked her dad. "I like to plant them, but I don't like to eat them."

"Beets have lots of nutrients that help our bodies and fight off disease," explained her dad. "Vegetables of all kinds are important for us to eat."

"I like peas and carrots," Leena said, "but what I really like is candy!"

"Maybe we should plant some candy in our garden and see if it comes up," suggested her dad with a grin.

In today's Bible story, we learn that people brought their little children to Jesus so he would bless them. The parents knew Jesus was special, and wanted their children to be part of the family of God.

The disciples didn't understand that it's important to take time for all people, including babies and children. But Jesus understood. He knew that people of all ages have gifts they can offer to God.

When parents tell us to eat our veggies, they know what they are talking about. When they take us to church and teach us about God, our parents show how important it is for all of us to be part of God's family.

What are your favorite vegetables?

What does it mean for you to follow Jesus?

Come and See*

"Come and see, come and see,
I am the way and the truth," said He.
"Follow Me, Follow Me,
Come as a child, O come and see."

Christe, Christe,
Adoramus te.
Alleluia,
Kyrie eleison.[1]

—Marilyn Houser Hamm

[1] Latin: Christ, Christ, we worship you. Alleluia, Lord, have mercy.

LET US PRAY

Dear Jesus, thank you for giving us parents who know what is best for us. Thank you for stretching out your arms to welcome us all into God's family. Amen.

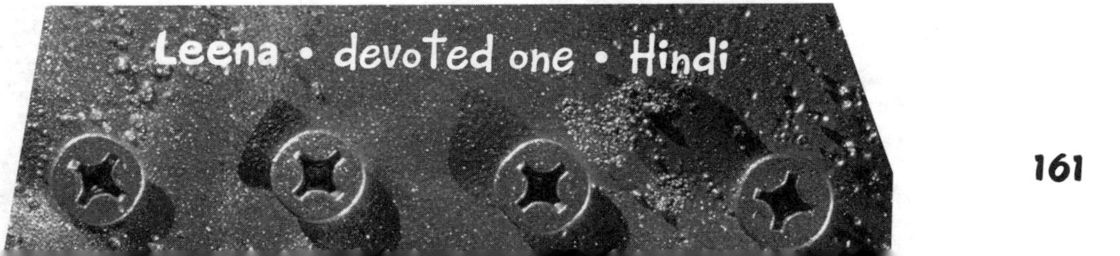

78

Feeding Pets

READ
Luke 20:21-25

Give . . . to God the things that are God's.
—Luke 20:25b

Pancho's neighbors were gone for the weekend, and he had promised to take care of their house. They had a lot of pets—dogs, cats, rabbits, turtles, ferrets, and guinea pigs.

Pancho had visited the pets before, but he'd never fed them. Unfortunately, the neighbors had not left clear instructions. Pancho had to try his best to figure out which pets got which food.

"Would it help if you looked at the animal pictures on the bags of food?" his stepdad asked.

"Oh, I never thought of that," Pancho replied. "Thanks."

We have to remember many things when we feed and care for pets. We give them the food they need to live, and we give them comfortable shelters.

Jesus tells us to give to the government what is the government's and to give to God what is God's. How do we decide what belongs to the government and what belongs to God? Could we give cat food to the government and rabbit food to God? That would be silly.

But we do make decisions each day about how we will use our money. We pay taxes to our government, and we hope the people in the government will use the money to make our country and our world a better place for all.

We also give money to God when we contribute to the work of the church. But we give God more than money. In our worship we give praise and honor to God. Since God, our Creator, is far greater than any government here on earth, we give our hearts—our whole selves—to God.

What kind of taxes does your family pay?

When does your family give money to God?

Grant Us, Lord, the Grace*

Grant us, Lord, the grace of giving,
With a spirit large and free,
That ourselves and all our living
We may offer unto thee.
—Anonymous

LET US PRAY.

Dear Lord of our lives, we love you far more than we love anything here on earth. Help us to know how to use our money wisely. In your holy name we pray. Amen.

Pancho • plume • Spanish

79

Cross Gift

READ
Luke 23:44-47

The message about the cross . . . is the power of God.
—1 Corinthians 1:18

When Vicky's family received a package in the mail, they wondered what it could be. "Is it a gift, or do we have to pay for it?" Vicky asked.

"I don't know what it is," her mom replied, "but it's probably something pretty special if it's from your uncle."

Sure enough, when Vicky unwrapped the package and pulled out all the Styrofoam packing, she found a beautiful gift: a clear, acrylic cross with a picture of Jesus inside it.

"Why do we always see Jesus on the cross?" Vicky asked. "Didn't he ever get down from it?"

We often see pictures of Jesus on the cross. For 2,000 years famous artists have shown Jesus on the cross. But why? What is so important about Jesus dying?

We are Christians because of Jesus Christ, God's Son. Jesus came to our earth, lived here, died on the cross, and rose from the dead. The cross has become a way for us to remember his power over death. It reminds us that Jesus died so that we and all people can be close to God.

Jesus is no longer on the cross. He's alive and waiting in heaven for you and me. Still, Jesus' death gave us the beautiful gift of life. We don't have to pay for that life—it is a very special gift.

What questions do you have about Jesus?

What does the cross teach us?

LET US PRAY

Dear Jesus, thank you for caring enough about each of us to die on the cross so that we might live forever and ever. Amen.

For God So Loved the World*

For God so loved the world
He gave his only Son
To die on Calv'ry's tree
From sin to set me free;
Some day he's coming back—
What glory that will be!
Wonderful his love to me.
—Frances Townsend

Vicky (Victoria) • winner, Conqueror • Latin

80

Jesus Bridge

READ
Luke 24:50-53

While he was blessing them, he withdrew from them and was carried up into heaven.
—Luke 24:51

Céleste felt on top of the world as she rode with her dad in his truck. She had been with him all day, and they were heading home. "The bridge is ahead," her dad said, alerting Céleste to her favorite part of the trip.

Céleste loved bridges. She especially liked the suspension bridges that her dad had taught her about. They seemed to hang in the air, and she was amazed that anyone would know how to build a bridge like that.

Sometimes, as she went over a bridge, Céleste would try to imagine a world without bridges. How could the roads get to where they were going? she wondered.

Many of us go over bridges almost every day. They link us with people and places on the other side.

Jesus was like a bridge between heaven and earth. He carried God's good news from God to people. After his resurrection, when his earthly work was done, he went back to heaven. This story of Jesus is often called the Ascension.

As Christians, we too are on the road to heaven. Like the disciples, we feel Jesus blessing us as we do God's work on earth. We worship Jesus. We are joyful. Like the disciples, we share the good news about Jesus with other travelers here on earth.

Whenever you go over a bridge this week, say "Praise God."

What kind of bridges do you know about?

Why is it important that the disciples saw Jesus ascend (or go up) to heaven?

LET US PRAY

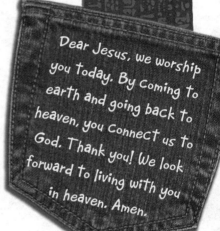

Dear Jesus, we worship you today. By coming to earth and going back to heaven, you connect us to God. Thank you! We look forward to living with you in heaven. Amen.

Worship for Ascension Day

To honor Jesus' ascension to heaven, worship together as a family on Ascension Day, 40 days after Easter.

- Walk to a quiet spot outdoors, and name it your Mount of Olives.
- Read a Bible passage, such as Luke 24:50-52, Acts 1:9-11, Psalm 47, John 14:1-4, Matthew 28:16-20.
- Offer written or spoken prayers, celebrating Jesus' return to heaven.
- Bless each family member with these words: _________ (name), you are God's child here on earth. You have gifts of _________ (name the person's gifts, talents) to use in serving others. May God bless you this day and give you peace. Amen."

- Blow soap bubbles to represent Jesus going to heaven.
- Sing the song below to the tune of "If You're Happy and You Know It:"

If you want to worship Jesus, clap your hands, (clap, clap)
If you want to worship Jesus, clap your hands, (clap, clap)
If you see him lifted high so he touches heaven's sky,
Then you'll want to worship Jesus. Clap your hands. (clap, clap)
—J.G.K.

Céleste • heavenly • French

81

Peace Faces

READ
John 14:1-3

Peace I leave with you; my peace I give to you. . . . Do not let your hearts be troubled, and do not let them be afraid.
—John 14:27

As Reyna stood at the sink washing dishes, she was unusually quiet. "A penny for your thoughts," said her mom, who was cleaning up the kitchen. Reyna's mom always seemed to know when something was bothering Reyna.

"I'm afraid you might have to have surgery," Reyna said. "I can't help thinking about the terrible pains you've had lately."

Reyna's mom didn't seem worried. "There are worse things than surgery, and God will be with you and me no matter what happens."

Sicknesses and worries about the future can make us and others in our family afraid. When troubles pile up, our faces can look as messy as dirty dishes.

Jesus promises us peace. When we are afraid or worried, Jesus promises to be with us. When we trust Jesus, God brings us the gift of peace, because we know that everything will be okay.

When your heart is troubled, turn to Jesus and ask him to give you the peace he gave his disciples.

Joy is the daughter of peace.
—Finnish proverb

How does your face look when you are afraid?

How does your face look when Jesus' peace is shining in you?

LET US PRAY

O God of peace, we
turn to you today.
Wipe away our
worries and fears.
Let us shine for you.
Amen.

Pour the Peace

Pour the peace of Christ upon me
like a lotion to my worries.
Let your presence and compassion
rest upon me through my hurries.

When I'm troubled and afraid,
and I don't know where I'm going,
hold my hands if you are able;
sit beside me at the table.
Pour the peace of Christ on me.

—J.G.K.

(can be sung to tune of
"My soul is filled with joy"* SJ 13)

Reyna • peaceful • Spanish

82

READ

Acts 2:42-47

All who believed were together.
—Acts 2:44

Lots of Knots

When was the last time you tied a knot? *(Wait for responses; then review "Uses for knots" on the next page.)*

For several thousand years people have used knots to make their lives easier and more enjoyable. Knots are especially important to climbers and sailors, but all of us need to know how to tie some knots.

Strings, yarns, ropes, threads, and fibers—it's amazing what they can do. They tie, bend, twist, loop, bind, and fasten. People tie them into many kinds of knots. Common ones are the figure-eight, the overhand, and the bow knot. Good strings and ropes make good knots that can last a long time.

Like the early Christians who came together in fellowship, we know it is important to meet regularly with other Christians. Our love for God and our eagerness to follow Jesus ties us together tightly.

As a church we do many things together. We sing and pray. We study the Bible. We care for people who are hurting. We play and celebrate together. We tell others about Jesus. All of these activities are the knots that hold us together.

Good knots make the church strong. When we're tied tightly to God's family here and around the world, God can use us in mighty ways. The next time you tie a knot, think of God's church that binds us together.

How do you work with your hands to help others?

What do you like to do when you are together with other Christians?

Uses for knots

camping
mountain-climbing
crocheting
farming
fishing
friendship bracelets
games
lacemaking
lariats
mathematics
neckties
rugs
sailing
scarves
sewing
shoelaces
surgery
tree-climbing
trucking

LET US PRAY

(Ask listeners to hold hands during the prayer.) Bind us together, Lord, so that we can be a strong family of faith. As we are tied with you, help us also to be tied to other Christians. Amen.

83

Be Bold

READ
Acts 4:29-31

When they saw the boldness of Peter and John and realized they were uneducated and ordinary men, they were amazed and recognized them as companions of Jesus. —Acts 4:13

Dana had trouble reading aloud. Some words, like lose, loose, and loss all looked so much the same that he would pause before reading them. Words he'd never seen before also made him stop reading.

Even when his teacher was the only one listening, Dana was embarrassed. He just couldn't say the words right. So he would read very softly.

"Be bold," his teacher told him.

"What do you mean?" Dana whispered.

"Reading comes with lots and lots of practice," the teacher replied, "and you can't practice if you don't read. Being bold means taking a risk."

We sometimes envy people who can speak or read aloud without making mistakes. If we're shy, then reading or speaking aloud can seem extra hard.

Peter and John were uneducated and ordinary disciples of Jesus. But they knew what to say and they said it boldly even though they were beaten and told not to speak in public about Jesus. They prayed with the church, asking God for boldness for everyone else in the church, and God answered their prayers.

God wants us to be bold in telling others about Jesus. God wants us to be confident Christians. Even if we sometimes make mistakes, say the wrong words, or don't know quite what to say, God gives us the strength to be as bold as Peter and John.

When have you been sad or afraid?

How might God be asking you to be bold?

I'm Gonna Sing When the Spirit Says

1. I'm gonna sing when the spirit says sing,
I'm gonna sing when the spirit says sing,
I'm gonna sing when the spirit says sing,
And obey the spirit of the Lord.

2. I'm gonna shout . . .

3. I'm gonna pray . . .

—African-American Spiritual

LET US PRAY.

Dear God, we want to tell others about Jesus. We want to be as bold as Peter and John. Fill us with your Spirit. In your name we pray. Amen.

BE BOLD

Be strong and bold;
have no fear or dread . . .
because it is the LORD your God
who goes with you.
—Moses (Deuteronomy 31:6)

Dana • God is my judge • Czech

84

Table Decision

READ
Acts 4:32-35

Bear one another's burdens.
—Galatians 6:2

Usually, when Mariko and her family shopped at the mall, they went in different directions. This time was different. Their mother wanted them all to help buy a new dining table and chairs. Even Gramps came along in his wheelchair.

"We're a big family," their mother said. "We have to find a table that works for all of us, and we need to agree on the decision."

"Did you bring along your dogs?" Gramps asked Mariko with a twinkle in his eye. "What if Duke and Daisy don't fit beneath the table we choose?"

Families share lots of things, including tables, chairs, and pets. Our clothes, our toothbrushes, and many of our toys only belong to one person. But a lot of other possessions belong to the whole family.

The early Christians were like one big family and did a good job of sharing what they had with others in their church. Acts 4 tells us that everything they had they owned together. No one needed anything because the community took care of everyone's needs.

Today when we help those who are needy in our church, it's as if we are all sitting around one big table, sharing what we have with everyone. We do this because of Jesus, who taught us to not be selfish and to care for others.

What things do you have a hard time sharing with others?

How does your church care for people?

Sharing

I'm so glad that people share
When I need their help and care.
They're so glad that I can share
When they need my help and care.
—J.G.K.

LET US PRAY

Dear Lord Jesus, thank you for teaching us to care about others. Help us to be more willing to share what we have. Amen.

Sharing as a family goal

Sharing happens when people allow time to care for others—either as families or as churches. Talk about ways you can use the gifts and talents God has given you to help those in need. What can you share? Make a list of all the things that your family can share with others. Try to think of a few things that you can't see or touch.

Mariko • Circle • Japanese

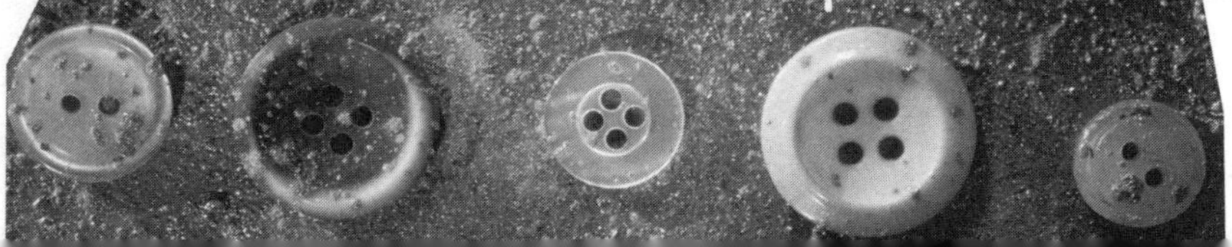

85

Second Chance

READ
Acts 9:26-28

Be at peace among yourselves.
—1 Thessalonians 5:13

"He takes things he's not supposed to," Travis told his mom. "I don't have to be friends with him. He said he won't do it again, but I know he will." The bright sun poured through the car window and onto Travis, but he didn't feel very sunny at all.

"You can give him a second chance," she said. "He returned your watch."

"Mom, you don't know what he's like. He's sneaky, and what he says doesn't always match up with what he does."

"This time it might," she said. "Give him a chance to be better."

It's hard to know when we can trust people. When they take things from us or don't tell the truth, it's hard to be friends with them.

In Acts 9 the disciples had a hard time accepting Saul. Jesus had appeared to Saul in a blinding light, calling him to a new life. But the disciples didn't see that. They just remembered the bad things he had done. Could they really trust Saul?

Barnabas thought so. Barnabas gave Saul the chance he needed to prove he could be trusted. And because of Barnabas, Saul went on to become a very important church leader and missionary.

God gives all of us second chances, and we can do the same for others. When we goof up or when others let us down, God shows us how to make new starts.

What do you think Travis will do?

When has God given you a second chance?

LET US PRAY

Dear God, it's hard to be good. Give us a second chance so we can do the same to others. Amen.

From Saul to Paul, from near to far

The Saul in today's Bible story is the same person as the Apostle Paul. Saul was his Jewish name. Paul, his Roman name, was used more when he and the church began mission work among Jews and Gentiles. Paul means "small," but the work he did to spread the news of Jesus Christ was huge.

Test your knowledge of the places that were important to Paul. Which can you find on a world map? (Answers are on page 209)

1. Saul/Paul was born in: a. Tarsus; b. Thessalonica; c. Tucson; d. Timbuktu (see Acts 21:39).

2. Paul became a follower of Jesus on the road to: a. Damascus; b. the Dead Sea; c. Durham; d. Durango (see Acts 9:3).

3. Because of Paul, the disciples were first called Christians in the city of: a. Antioch; b. Athens; c. Aberdeen; d. Alexandria (see Acts 11:25-26).

4. After a bad storm at sea, Paul and others finally reached an island called: a. Malta; b. Mykonos; c. Maui; d. Madagascar (see Acts 28:1).

5. Paul wrote many letters that are now part of our Bible. He wrote the Letter of Romans to the Christians in: a. Rome; b. Rhodes; c. Red Lake; d. Rio De Janeiro (see Romans 1:7).

Travis • Crossroads • French

86

Miracle Sister

READ
Acts 9:32-35

Jesus Christ heals you; get up.
—Acts 9:34

Shani's adopted sister Tabia is a miracle. At least, that's what Shani's parents often say.

Tabia was so tiny when she was born that the doctors didn't think she could live. She stayed in the hospital a long time because at first she couldn't breathe on her own. When she came to live with Shani's family, Tabia couldn't see very well. She had to get glasses even when she was little.

Now, at age four, she acts like all the other kids in Shani's family. Shani doesn't even think of her as adopted. She feels Tabia is a real sister and loves her a lot.

We can't make miracles happen. But sometimes God surprises us with them. Sometimes people who are very sick recover without doctors or medicines to help them. Children with no place to live find loving homes.

A miracle is something that happens that we can't explain completely through science. It's something that causes us to wonder. A miracle helps us realize there is a God who is much greater than we are. Miracles remind us how much God cares for us. Jesus' birth is one of the greatest miracles we know.

"Jesus Christ heals you," Peter said to Aeneas. Jesus had given Peter and the other disciples the power to perform miracles, like healing the sick. Today, too, Jesus gives us power to grow and learn and to do God's work. Sometimes we might see big miracles, such as Tabia's healing. But we also see smaller miracles that remind us of God's greatness and love.

What good things has God done for you?

What miracles is God doing today?

LET US PRAY

Dear God, thank you for the miracles you make happen every day, including the miracle of life. Help us to notice your miracles in our lives. Amen.

To me every hour of the light and dark
is a miracle,
Every cubic inch of space
is a miracle.
—Walt Whitman

Shani • marvelous • Swahili
Tabia • talented • Swahili

87

READ
Acts 11:27-30

Always seek to do good to one another and to all.
—1 Thessalonians 5:15 International Children's Bible

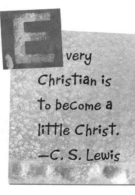

Every Christian is to become a little Christ.
—C. S. Lewis

Hairdryer Storm

"Look out," Kris yelled from the bathroom, just after his bath. "Here comes a big storm."

"Where?" asked his baby sister, pretending to be worried.

"Right here," he announced with a big voice. In his hand was the hairdryer, blowing warm air in front of him. He aimed it at the houses he'd made of playing cards earlier in the evening, just outside the bathroom door. SWOOSH. In an instant they collapsed onto the floor.

Real storms and other acts of nature can leave an even bigger mess than the one Kris made. Sometimes we hear news about hurricanes or earthquakes that destroy people's homes. Other times we hear about people who don't have enough food because there hasn't been enough rain.

In the book of Acts, we read about a place called Antioch, where Jesus' followers were first called Christians. The disciples there heard that many people in Jerusalem didn't have enough food to eat. They decided to help by sending food to them.

Today, when storms, wars, or droughts make a mess, who cleans up? As Christians, we believe that Jesus wants us to help people even if we don't know them. We help by giving money, packing relief kits, sending food or clothing, or helping to clean up after a disaster. Like the first Christians, we want to do our part to help people who can't help themselves.

When have you helped people you didn't know?

What could you do this week to help someone far away?

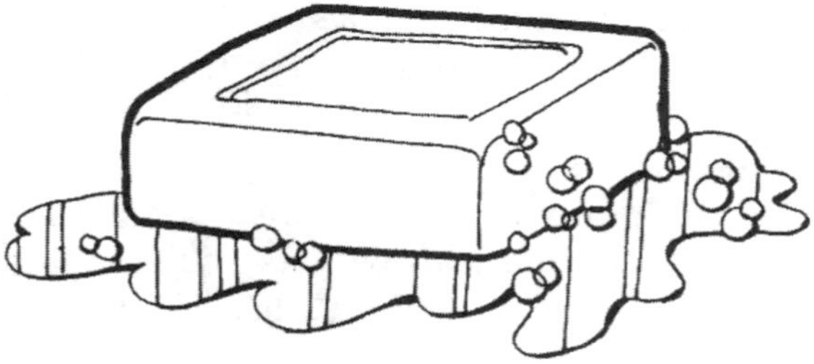

LET US PRAY

Dear Jesus, we know that you help us when we have messes in our lives. Now, we pray that you will help us be generous to others. Amen.

Let Me Pick the Flowers

Let me pick the flowers that you need today;
Let me gather daisies to sweep the pain away.
When the storm is over and when the sun shines bright,
Let me find some flowers to help you through the night.

Let me hear you crying when you weep today;
Bombs and wars and hatred won't sweep the pain away.
When the storm is over and when the Son shines bright,
I will wipe your tears to make the wrongs all right.

—J.G.K.

Kris • Christ-bearer • Swedish

88

Skateboard Launch

READ
Acts 13:1-5

[Jesus said,] Go . . . and make disciples of all nations.
—Matthew 28:19

Jeremiah sat up in bed. Yes, his new skateboard was exactly where he had left it before he went to sleep. He could hardly wait for his first go on it. When he'd unwrapped the huge present the night before, he wanted to ride on the board right then. But he couldn't because the sky was too dark and stormy.

Jeremiah dressed quickly, but took enough time to put on the knee and elbow pads and helmet. On his way out the door, he flew past his parents and grandparents. They were already up to watch his first ride.

"Hey, world, here I come!" Jeremiah yelled.

Getting presents and trying out new things is like an adventure into a new world, especially when the presents have wheels.

In Acts 13 the early Christians were on their own kind of new ride. As they worshipped together, they felt the Holy Spirit calling Saul and Barnabas to a new job. The two set sail to take the good news about Jesus to countries where people had never heard about Jesus.

What kind of ride are we on? As Christians, we have the energy of God's Spirit to help us get the good news about Jesus to those who need it. Jesus tells us to "go." For now, that's just down the street and around the corner. When we're older, God may call us to go much farther. Wherever we go, people will be waiting to hear about Jesus and see God's love working through us. Will we be ready to carry God's mission across the street and around the world?

Who does God want you to talk with this week?

What is the good news about Jesus?

God's Love Is for Everybody*

God's love is for everybody,
Everyone around the world,
Me and you and all God's children
From across the street to around the world,
From across the street to around the world.
—Bryan Moyer Suderman

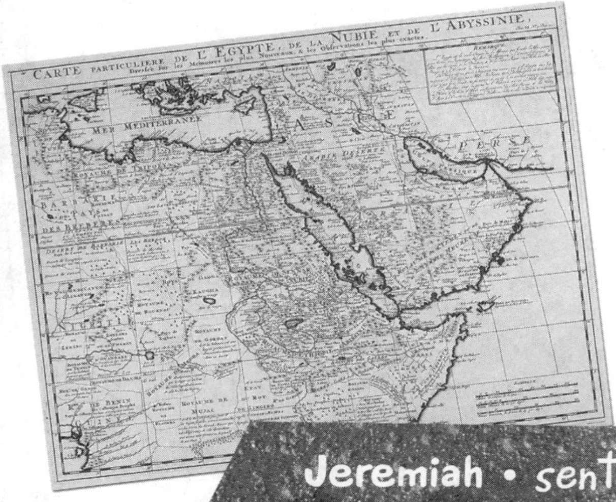

LET US PRAY.

Dear Lord, because you have found us, we too want to launch your mission. Let us be the wheels that will take your good news everywhere. Amen.

Jeremiah • sent by God • Hebrew

89

Computer Conflict

READ
Acts 15:36-41

Agree with one another, live in peace; and the God of love and peace will be with you.
—2 Corinthians 13:11b

The computer wasn't working right. Noah and Geoffrey both needed to use it, and each thought he knew how to make it work better. Their little disagreement turned into a big one. Soon Noah walked out of the room and slammed the door.

"I don't have to listen to him," he muttered.

After a few minutes Geoffrey stuck his head out the door. "Come on, Noah, let's work this out."

Conflicts are a normal part of life, and every family has them. While some quarreling and anger can lead to bitterness and hatred that last a long time, the little disagreements that most families experience can be resolved easily and quickly.

In today's Bible story we read about two friends, Paul and Barnabas, who had a big disagreement. Their solution was for both of them to go different directions in their missionary travels.

God can help us when we feel like slamming the door during an argument. If we are willing, God can help us find the words we need to say that will help us solve the problem.

In your family, what do you argue about the most?

Think of a conflict you may be in now.
What would God like you to do to bring peace?

LET US PRAY

God of Peace, we turn to you because you are the one who knows how we can make things better. Forgive us when we fight. Guide us as we work through our disagreements. Amen.

How to work out conflicts fairly and peacefully*

1. STOP—before you lose control of your temper and make the conflict worse.
2. SAY—what you feel is the problem. What is causing the disagreement? What do you want?
3. LISTEN—to the other person's ideas and feelings.
4. THINK—of solutions that will satisfy both of you.

If you still can't agree, ask someone else to help you work it out.

You must first get along with yourself before you can get along with others.
—Anthony D'Angelo

Geoffrey • gift of peace • English

Noah • rest, peace • Hebrew

90

READ
Acts 16:11–15

[Jesus] said, . . . "Come, follow me."
—Luke 18:22

Yellow Shirts

Angelina's family often dressed alike when they went places where there were lots of people. Mom believed that if one of them got separated from the others, the matching shirts would help them find each other again.

Today, on a trip to an amusement park, Angelina's family and her cousins and uncle wore bright yellow shirts.

"Since you have never been to this park, let's stay together the whole time," their uncle said as they approached the entry gate. "We'll play Follow the Leader all day."

Often it makes good sense to follow others and stick together, especially when we don't know where we are going.

Our Bible story tells about Lydia, who learned from Paul what it meant to be a follower of Jesus. As she spent time with Paul and his companions, Paul's teaching changed her.

We, too, learn about Jesus from people we know. Often they are older than we are—people like our parents or grandparents or other adults. We trust them to lead us and help us understand Bible lessons we don't know.

In life, we don't follow someone's example because of the color of shirt the person is wearing. What is important is whether the person knows and follows Jesus' teachings.

Who do you follow and why?

What is one important thing that Jesus taught us?

Following Jesus from A to Z

The Bible gives us many tips on how to follow Jesus. Look up some or all of the verses below, and feel free to add others.

Accept instruction. —Proverbs 19:20
Believe in the resurrection. —Romans 10:9
Confess the truth openly. —James 5:16
Do what is right. —2 Thessalonians 3:13
Encourage others. —1 Thessalonians 4:18
Forgive one another. —Ephesians 4:32
Give cheerfully. —2 Corinthians 9:7
Help the weak. —1 Thessalonians 5:14
Imitate what is good. —3 John 1:11
Be **J**oyful always. —1 Thessalonians 5:16
Be **K**ind to one another. —Ephesians 4:32
Love your enemies. —Matthew 5:44
Make music to the Lord. —Ephesians 5:19
Never give up. —Galatians 6:9
Offer praise to God. —Hebrews 13:15
Pray without stopping. —1 Thessalonians 5:17
Be **Q**uick to listen. —James 1:19
Remember Jesus. —Luke 22:19
Share with others. —Hebrews 13:16
Thank God for everything. —Ephesians 5:20
Unite with one another. —1 Corinthians 1:10
Visit the sick and the prisoner. —Matthew 25:36
Welcome others. —Romans 15:7
Go the e**X**tra mile. —Matthew 5:41
Yearn to worship. —Psalms 84:2
Zealously serve the Lord. —Romans 12:11

LET US PRAY

Dear Jesus, open our hearts so we can listen and change to be more like you. Thank you for the people who teach us about you. Amen.

Love the Lord your God with all your heart, and with all your soul, and with all your mind, and with all your strength. . . . Love your neighbor as yourself.
—Mark 12:30-31

Angelina • little angel • Italian

91

Tree House

READ
Acts 18:1-3

In all the work you are doing, work the best you can.
—Colossians 3:23
International Children's Bible

Up. Up. Up. Mason, Tanner, and Penny worked every Saturday on their tree house. The steps up were hard to make, but with their neighbor's guidance, they figured it out. Then came the floor and the walls. Each day they could see the tree house taking shape.

One day as they hammered their last nails, they heard a soft voice from below. "I'd like to talk with you when you're done up there." It was the elderly woman from across the alley. "My fence is falling apart. I could use your help if you can work some more."

There are many ways we work with and for others. Sometimes work brings together people who have the same kind of jobs. Adults often partner together in business to earn money. Work also brings together those who know Jesus, when they cooperate on projects that help others.

The apostle Paul learned to know Priscilla and Aquila, and they became friends. They all believed in God and followed Jesus, but they also made tents for a living. While they made tents, they also taught others about Jesus.

Mason, Tanner, and Penny's work on the tree house took them up, up, up to see the world beyond. In the same way, our work for others can help us see the world through God's eyes.

What kind of work do you enjoy most?

When have you done work to help others?

LET US PRAY

Dear God, thank you for jobs we do each day in our homes and communities. Help us honor you in all we do. Amen.

In Our Work and in Our Play

In our work and in our play,
Jesus, ever with us stay;
May we always strive to be
True and faithful unto thee.
Then we truthfully can sing,
We are children of the King.

—Whitfield G. Wills

Mason • stone worker • French

Penny (Penelope) • weaver • Greek

Tanner • leather worker • German

92

Watercolor God

READ
Romans 15:1-2, 5-6

Patience and encouragement come from God. And I pray that God will help you all agree with each other the way Christ Jesus wants. —Romans 15:5 International Children's Bible

"This is God," Kalinda announced one day as she began to paint with watercolors. In the middle of the paper she painted a big red circle.

"How do you know that's God?" asked her little brother Nathan.

"It just is," Kalinda said. She cleaned her brush in the water and dipped it in green paint. "These are people," she announced, dabbing smaller circles of paint around the big one. She added more circles in various colors.

Soon, the paints began to run together. "It looks like God and all the people are trying to get together," Nathan said. "What do you call that?" he asked.

When people meet with God, that's called worship. The best worship happens when all the worshippers live in harmony with one another.

The verses we read from Romans 15 tell us to be tolerant of others, to build each other up, and to glorify God with one voice.

As Christians, we care about others. When we do, we understand better what it means to worship God. And when we worship God, then we understand better what it means to care about others.

What does it mean to care for people in your home?

What does it mean to care about God?

Tuck Me in with God

When I pray,
Wrap me in Heaven.
Tuck me in with God
Right here beside me,
Jesus, my soft Pillow,
The Spirit, my Comforter.
Then my feet are warm.
—J.G.K.

LET US PRAY

Dear God, you are the One we worship. Thank you for putting us in families and in churches. Help us to know how to live together better. Amen.

We have watercolor moments every day whenever we absorb God's love. —J.G.K.

Kalinda • The sun • Hindi

Nathan • gift from God • Hebrew

93

Solid Foundation

READ
1 Corinthians 3:10-11

You are . . .
God's building.
—1 Corinthians 3:9b

Jesse and Makayla built a playhouse, draping old bed sheets over some card tables. But the playhouse refused to stay up. Every time the two went through their pretend door, the slippery sheets slid to the floor.

They worked a long time trying to get the sheets to cooperate. Zach heard their grumblings and came to their rescue. "You don't have anything holding down the corners," Zach said.

The children found some heavy books to hold the corners of the sheets on the floor.

Any construction project, like a big building or a small toothpick house, can fall apart if the bottom is weak. A solid building needs a solid foundation.

The same is true for our faith. In our reading for today, the writer Paul compares the church to a building that God makes. Paul is not talking about the boards and bricks that we use in our church buildings. He's talking about the people who make up the church. And the foundation, he says, is Jesus.

Love, trust, and honesty, are like the mortar that holds us together, like bricks in a building. With Jesus as the solid foundation on which we build our lives, we understand what it means to be one strong building together.

What kinds of things do you like to build or make?

How does your church have a strong foundation in Jesus?

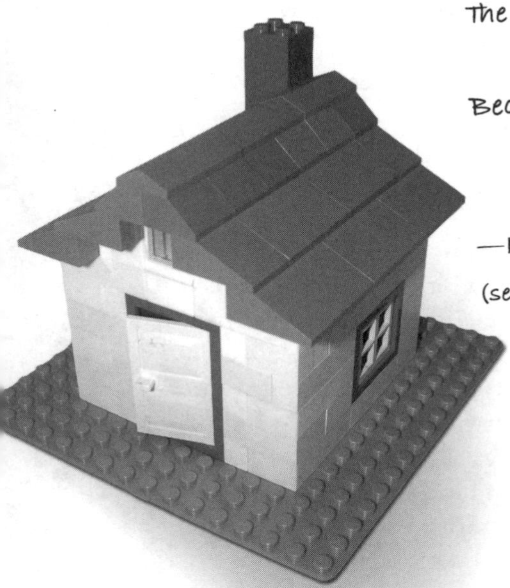

The Building Block

The building block
that was rejected
Became the cornerstone
of a whole new
world.
—Noel Paul Stookey
(see also 1 Peter 2:7)

LET US PRAY.

(Ask listeners to hold hands as leader prays this prayer and all repeat the Lord's Prayer.)

Dear Jesus, we believe in you and want to follow all your teachings. Help us to be strong Christians and strong churches because of you. Amen.

Jesse • God exists • Hebrew

Makayla • who is like God • Celtic/Gaelic

Zach (Zachariah) • God remembered • Hebrew

94

READ
1 Corinthians 13:4-7

Love is patient; love is kind; love is not envious or boastful or arrogant.
—1 Corinthians 13:4

Acting Love

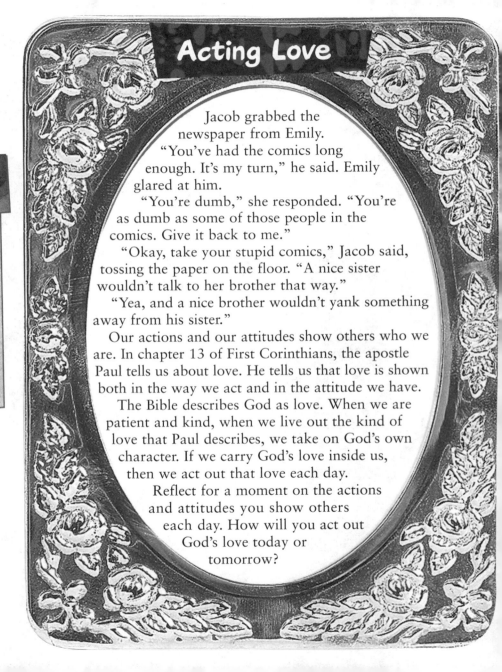

Jacob grabbed the newspaper from Emily. "You've had the comics long enough. It's my turn," he said. Emily glared at him.

"You're dumb," she responded. "You're as dumb as some of those people in the comics. Give it back to me."

"Okay, take your stupid comics," Jacob said, tossing the paper on the floor. "A nice sister wouldn't talk to her brother that way."

"Yea, and a nice brother wouldn't yank something away from his sister."

Our actions and our attitudes show others who we are. In chapter 13 of First Corinthians, the apostle Paul tells us about love. He tells us that love is shown both in the way we act and in the attitude we have.

The Bible describes God as love. When we are patient and kind, when we live out the kind of love that Paul describes, we take on God's own character. If we carry God's love inside us, then we act out that love each day.

Reflect for a moment on the actions and attitudes you show others each day. How will you act out God's love today or tomorrow?

Name one person you know who shows what real love is all about.

What have you learned about God's love recently?

May I so live the life of love this day
that all those with whom I have anything to do
may be as sure of love in the world
as they are of the sunlight.
—Unknown

LET US PRAY

Dear God of love, teach us to be patient and kind. Teach us everything you know about love. Help us to act out your love today. In your holy name, we pray. Amen.

Moun ki gen renmen nan kè li gen pasyans, li gen bon kè, li p'ap anvye sò lòt moun. Li p'ap fè grandizè, li p'ap gonfle ak lògèy.
—Haitian Creole

La charité est patiente, elle est pleine de bonté; la charité n'est point envieuse; la charité ne se vante point, elle ne s'enfle point d'orgueil.
—French

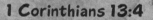

1 Corinthians 13:4

Miłość cierpliwa jest,
łaskawa jest.
Miłość nie zazdrości,
nie szuka poklasku,
nie unosi się pychą.
—Polish

El amor es sufrido, es benigno;
el amor no tiene envidia;
el amor no es jactancioso,no se envanece.
—Spanish

Emily • admiring • Latin

Jacob • substitute • Hebrew

95

Cheerful Giver

"Dad, I don't want to give away these toys. I still use them." Eva paused and then added, "Well, some of them I still use."

Eva's family was cleaning a closet. While her parents were ready to give away things they weren't using, Eva was a packrat. She wanted to keep every toy and every game she had ever played with.

"What do I get out of it if I give them away?" she asked.

Her dad insisted, "Since we're not using them, why not give them to other kids who can?"

Why do we give to others? Sometimes it's because we want to clean out our closets. But the main reason to give is because it helps others.

The Apostle Paul's friends in Corinth had not learned to give to help others. That is why, in his letter, Paul encouraged them to give generously. "God loves a cheerful giver," he wrote.

Giving only because we think we should takes away the spirit of true giving. Jesus also taught us not to give because we'll get something out of it. We give because we love God and others.

When we give joyfully and generously, we are sometimes surprised. Since it brings us joy, it seems we receive back far more than we think we have given! God wants us to give away our time, our money, and our possessions, and to do so generously and cheerfully.

READ 2 Corinthians 9:7–8

God loves a cheerful giver.
—2 Corinthians 9:7

It is in giving that we receive.
—St. Francis of Assisi

What have you received because of someone's generosity?

Why is giving an important part of being a Christian?

LET US PRAY

Dear God, you have given us so much, and we thank you. Because we have received, teach us new ways to give cheerfully this week. Amen.

Take My Life*

Take my life, and let it be
consecrated, Lord, to thee.
Take my moments and my days;
let them flow in ceaseless praise. . . .
—Frances R. Havergal

Eva • giver of life • Hebrew

96

READ
Ephesians 4:29, 31–5:2

Let no evil talk come out of your mouths, but only what is useful for building up.
—Ephesians 4:29

BUILDING WORDS

When Cody returned home after a long day at school, he found his dad in the garage. It was a perfect time to talk about the day.

"Every time I open my mouth, I get into trouble," Cody complained. He told his dad that at the end of basketball practice, he had made a wisecrack.

"Everyone else thought it was funny, but the coach bawled me out," Cody said angrily, throwing his bag onto the garage floor.

"Hold on," his dad said. "We need to talk about this. But right now it sounds like you need some cool-down time."

Many of us like it when people pay attention to our words, but what we say can sometimes get us into big trouble. Too often, we speak first and think later.

In the book of Ephesians, Paul reminds us to be careful with what we say—to "let no bad talk come out of our mouths."

Paul encourages us to say only what builds others up. He tells us to think less about ourselves and more about other people—to talk less and listen more. When we do so, we imitate God and are better able to live in love with those around us.

What words can you use to encourage someone else?

How can you imitate God this week?

LET US PRAY

Dear God, forgive us for saying words that harm others. Please help us learn to use words wisely. Help us to love others as you love us. Amen.

Guard your tongue in youth,
and in age you may mature a thought
that will be of service
to your people.
—Wabashaw, Dakota chief*

Whatever comes from God also leads to God.
—David Beiler*

Cody • a cushion • English

97

READ
Colossians 3:12-17

Just as the Lord has forgiven you, so you also must forgive.
—Colossians 3:13

Sunburn Sorry

"Mommy, I'm so sorry," Erin said, clinging to her mother and sobbing. "You told me not to stay out in the sun too long, and I did anyway. Now my skin hurts so bad. I forgot to help Grammy, and I didn't set the table for supper, and now you're late for your meeting. I'm sorry!"

"I forgive you, and I'm hurting because you are," her mother said. She rubbed cooling salve on Erin's hot skin.

Erin hurt outside because of her sunburn. But she also hurt inside because she had disobeyed. Erin's mother knew that saying, "I'm sorry," and acting like it can start to make the pain go away. She also knew Erin needed to hear words of forgiveness to bring an end to pain and wrong.

The writer Paul knew all about forgiveness. His words call us to be patient when it's hard for us to accept other people's behavior. Paul teaches us to say "it's okay" when others hurt us and then say they're sorry. He calls us to love others and to be at peace.

What ideas would you have for making Erin feel better?

Is God nudging you to forgive someone today?

Forgiveness is a door to peace and happiness. It is a small, narrow door and cannot be entered without stooping.
—Johann Christoph Arnold

LET US PRAY

(Ask listeners to say "Forgive me" after each phrase you read.)

Loving Lord and forgiving God, for wrongs I have done this week,

All: Forgive me.

For words I have said that have caused pain,

All: Forgive me.

For actions I've done that have hurt someone,

All: Forgive me.

For things that I did not do or say that I should have done or said,

All: Forgive me.

I thank you because you always care for me, and you always

All: Forgive me.

Amen.

Erin • peace, Ireland • Irish

98

Long Run

READ
1 Timothy
4:6–10, 12

Train yourself in godliness.
—1 Timothy 4:7

"Hey, wait up," Brianna shouted to her sister. Brianna gasped for breath. Long-distance running was much harder than she thought it would be. Every muscle was telling her to stop.

Briana's sister slowed down only a little. "Don't think about the pain," she yelled back. "Think about the end. Think about crossing the finish line. Think about the celebration."

With sweat stinging her eyes, Brianna tried once more to catch up with her sister. "It's hard to think about the end when I'm still training my feet to think about the here and now," she mumbled to herself.

People who exercise regularly know the good feeling of a healthy body and mind. The Apostle Paul also knew how important exercise was. He must have been a sports fan. He praised athletes for their self-discipline. He knew that in order to win, athletes must work hard each day and compete by the rules.

Paul wrote to Timothy, saying, "Put the same effort into being godly as the athlete puts into preparing for competition."

Being godly means putting into practice everything we know about following God, right to the end of our lives. It involves spiritual exercises—spending time with God in prayer, reading the Bible, worshipping with other Christians, and taking God with us everywhere we go.

Paul says the Christian life is like a race. At the end there is a prize for those who cross the finish line. So let's keep doing our exercises!

What is your favorite sports event?

Use a sports term to describe God. (Example: God is like the mat we land on—always there to protect us.)

"Hope" is the thing with feathers
That perches in the soul
And sings the tune without the words
And never stops at all.
—Emily Dickinson

LET US PRAY

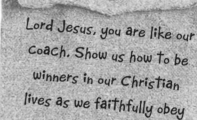

Lord Jesus, you are like our Coach. Show us how to be winners in our Christian lives as we faithfully obey you each day. Amen.

Brianna • strong one • Celtic/Gaelic

99

Echo Words

READ 2 Timothy 2:23-25a

Pursue righteousness, faith, love, and peace. —2 Timothy 2:22

Tameka and Tobias were twins, but they always seemed to be fighting with words. An argument would start over a silly disagreement. Within a short time one would say something that would make the other really angry.

Back and forth the words went. Often, one would just repeat the nasty comment the other said, only louder. They argued so much that their dad joked that he might put tape over their mouths. "If you stop saying nasty things to each other, they won't come back to you," he told the twins.

How would your words sound if they echoed back to you all the time? Would you like what you heard?

Our words have great power. We can use them to fight, tease, and criticize, or we can use them to praise, approve, and compliment. Once we say them, we can't get them back.

In his second letter to Timothy, Paul shows how well he knows the power of words. He writes: "Avoid wrangling over words, which does no good but only ruins those who are listening." (2 Timothy 2:14) Don't quarrel, but be patient, Paul tells us. Be kind. Correct others with gentleness.

As we talk today, let's listen to what we say. Let's turn to God for help in using words that bring peace.

Words are like bullets; if they escape, you can't catch them again. —Senegalese proverb

What do you argue about with others in your family?

What words are good to use when you disagree with someone?

Let the words of my mouth
and meditation of my heart
be acceptable to you,
O LORD, my rock and my redeemer.
Amen. —Psalm 19:14

LET US PRAY.

We pray, O God, for gentleness when we talk to others in our home and wherever we go. Grant us the wisdom to be kind and loving. Amen.

PEACE

Afrikaans • vrede
Arabic • سلام (salaam)
Bosnian • Spokoj
Cheyenne • nanomonsetôtse
French • paix
German • der friede
Greek • Irini
Hawaiian • malu
Hebrew • שלום (shalom)
Hindi • चांति (shanti)
Hmong • kev sib haum xeeb
Italian • pace
Japanese • 平和 (Heiwa)
Korean • 평화 (Peoning Hwa)
Lakota • Wolakota
Navajo • hozo
Norwegian • fred
Polish • pokoj
Portugese • paz
Quechua • havca causai
Russian • Мир (mir)
Spanish • paz
Swahili • Amani
Turkish • Barýþ (baris)
Vietnamese • Hoa Binh
Zapotec • Layeni
Zulu • Ukuthula

Tameka • twin • Arabic

Tobias • God is great • Hebrew

100

God's Reunion

READ
Revelation 5:13

Amen! Blessing and glory and wisdom and thanksgiving and honor and power and might be to our God forever and ever! Amen!
—Revelation 7:12

On their way to a family reunion, Jasmine sat in the front seat, holding an angel food cake on her lap. Her mother chatted excitedly as she drove.

"There will be more singing and storytelling than you have ever heard in your whole life," Mom said. "And hugging. You might get squeezed so much, you'll disappear for a while!"

She laughed that great big laugh of hers, then continued.

"And there will be tables and tables of food, and relatives from lots and lots of places. . . ."

"And angels too?" Jasmine interrupted. "I'm expecting to see angels since I keep smelling this angel food cake."

The book of Revelation shows us God's wonderful plan for a new heaven and the new earth when all creation will be made new.

Then, all of the angels and all of God's people who have ever lived on earth will be together again, enjoying God's presence. It will be like one great big reunion. Imagine! Heaven will be full of singing and love and peace—forever and ever.

As we look forward to that time, we can bring a bit of heaven to earth now. When others experience our love, it shows them something of what heaven is like.

What blessings from God do you enjoy today?

What bits of heaven could you show others today?

What is heaven?

We'll never find heaven on a map. But the Bible uses the word heaven *in several different ways.*

- Heaven is all creation except for the earth (Genesis 1:1).
- Heaven is the spiritual home of God (Matthew 6:8) and the place where God's perfect will is done (Matthew 6:10). God's Son, Jesus, came from heaven (John 3:13) and returned to heaven after his resurrection (Acts 1:11).

- Heaven is our home too, a spiritual place that we cannot see or completely understand during our life on earth (2 Corinthians 5:6-9).
- The "kingdom of heaven" is the reign of Jesus, which starts right now in our lives (Matthew 3:2).
- As Christians, we eagerly look forward to a "new heaven" (Revelation 21:1) where we will live with God forever (Matthew 28:20).

LET US PRAY

O great God, we bow together to worship you. We want to show how important you are to us. May your love and peace go with us this day and always. Amen and Amen!

The Lord bless you and keep you;
the Lord make his face to shine upon you
and be gracious to you;
the Lord lift up his countenance upon you,
and give you peace.
—Numbers 6:24-26

Acknowledgments

Thank you to my husband, Perry, for supporting me through this project; to our daughter, Melanie, and her husband, Jason, for their edits and ideas; and to our son, Joel, for improving every page.

Thanks to Gary, Dorothy, Carol, Kay, Jordan, Phil, Lori, and Elizabeth for reading many pages. Thanks to Ky, Sarah, LaDonna, Tenise, Sonya, Robin, Michelle, Miranda, Carry, Valerie, and others for their help, prayers, and encouragement. Thanks also to Art's family for letting me use the true story of the sheep stranded in flood waters.

Thanks to editor Byron and to Faith & Life Resources for making this happen.

Thank you to children everywhere who have given me ideas.

Thank you to our wonderful God, the Author of all.

—June

Answer Page

6

Bible Families: 1. Mary, 2. Zebedee, 3. Martha, 4. Moses, 5. Jesse, 6. David, 7. Ruth, 8. Timothy, 9. Priscilla, 10. Zechariah

8

A-Z Puzzle: ape-baby, butterfly-caterpillar; deer-fawn, eagle-eaglet, frog-tadpole, goose-gosling, kangaroo-joey, lion-cub, monkey-infant, pig-piglet, quail-chick, rabbit-bunny, sheep-lamb, turkey-poult, viper-snakelet, yak-calf, zebra-foal

27

Our Sun: All statements are true.

51

Trees Puzzle: 1g, 2d, 3a, 4e, 5i, 6f, 7c, 8b, 9j, 10h

53

Disciple Questions: 1d, 2d, 3d 4d, 5a

85

Paul's Places: All answers are a.

Sources for Hymns and Copyrighted Material

Where no copyright of permission information is included in this book, the quotation is in public domain or, because of the brevity of the excerpt, is considered "fair use."

The hymnal acronyms used are:

HWB: *Hymnal: A Worship Book* (Elgin, IL: Brethren Press, Newton, KS: Faith & Life Press, and Scottdale, PA: Mennonite Publishing House, 1992)

SJ: *Sing the Journey* (Scottdale, PA: Faith & Life Resources, 2005)

SR: *Sing and Rejoice* (Scottdale, PA: Herald Press, 1979)

MH: *The Mennonite Hymnal* (Newton, KS: Faith & Life Press, and Scottdale, PA: Herald Press, 1969)

NOTE: The numbers indicated are the number of the devotionals, not the page numbers.

1 HWB 648. Morning Has Broken.

2 "The Street Car," in *The Music Hour First Book,* (Silver, Burdett and Co., 1936), 14-15.

6 From Randolph K. Sanders, *A Parent's Bedside Companion* (Scottdale and Waterloo: Herald Press, 1992), 142.

9 HWB 513. To Go to Heaven.

14 "God Loves a Picnic," song lyrics © 2001 Bryan Moyer Suderman. From the CD "God's Love is for Everybody: Songs of Faith for Small and Tall" by Bryan Moyer Suderman (Mennonite Church Canada/Faith and Life Resources, 2002), distributed by SmallTall Music (www.smalltall-music.com) and Herald Press (www.herald-press.com).

15 "This Is the Day," © 1967, 1980 Scripture in Song, administered by Maranatha! Music, 205 Avenida Fabricante. *Used with permission.* San Clemente CA 92672. All rights reserved.

20 HWB 429. Go Now in Peace. ©1976 Hinshaw Music, Inc., PO Box 470, Chapel Hill, NC 17514. *Used with permission.*

22 SJ 70. "Jesus You Have Called Us," © 2003 Doug Krehbiel and Jude Krehbiel, 1125 N. Ash, Newton KS 67114, 316-283-7351. Laotian translation by Kuaying Teng

24 HWB 119. Praise God from Whom All Blessings Flow.

28 HWB 86. Now Thank We All Our God.

31 HWB 544. When We Walk with the Lord.

35 "Can You Count the Stars?" *The Youth Hymnary* (Newton, KS: Faith and Life Press, 1956), 70.

38 HWB 355. Savior, Like a Shepherd Lead Us.

40 "Volume of Friendship," reprinted from April 5, 2005 issue of *Sojourners* Magazine. *Used with permission.*

"We Pray for Peace," © Ken Medema Music/ASCAP/Brier Patch Music. From *Songs for Renewal, edited by* Janet Lindeblad Janzen with Richard J. Foster (San Francisco: Harper, 1995), 84.

42 HWB 212. O Come, All Ye Faithful.

43 HWB 614. "In the Bulb There Is a Flower," verse 1. ©Hope Publishing Co.

44 SR 39. I Have Decided to Follow Jesus.

45 "Disciples in Training," song lyrics © 2002 Bryan Moyer Suderman. From the CD "God's Love is for Everybody: Songs of Faith for Small and Tall" by Bryan Moyer Suderman (Mennonite Church Canada/Faith and Life Resources, 2002), distributed by SmallTall Music (www.smalltallmusic.com) and Herald Press (www.heraldpress.com).

48 HWB 226. "You Are the Salt for the Earth," ©1986 by G.I.A. Publications, Inc. All rights reserved. G.I.A. Publications, 7404 S. Mason Ave., Chicago, IL 60638, 708-496-3800.

49 SJ 49. "Rain Down," verse 3 and chorus, by Jaime Cortez ©1993 GIA Publications, Inc. 7404 S. Mason Ave., Chicago, IL 60638, 800-GIA-1358 www.giamusic,com. *Used with permission.*

"Your Shoes" game, inspired by Lauri Berkenkamp and Steven C. Atkins in *"Because I said so!" Family squabbles and how to handle them* (Norwich, VT.: Nomad Press, 2003), 103.

50 Samuel Landis quote from "A Plan for Prayer" by J. Craig Haas, in *Readings from Mennonite Writings New and Old* (Intercourse, PA: Good Books, 1992), 297.

54 SR 31. "God's Family," ©1977 by Patricia Shelly. *Used with permission.*

70 HWB 377. "Healer of Our Every Ill," chorus and verse 3. ©1987 G.I.A. Publications, Inc., 7404 S. Mason Ave., Chicago, IL 60638.*Used with permission.*

71 HWB 348. "O Lord, Hear My Prayer." ©1982 Les Presses de Taize. Contact: G.I.A. Publications, Inc., 7404 S. Mason Ave., Chicago, IL 60638

74 From *Prayers, Praises and Thanksgivings*, compiled by Sandol Stoddard (New York: Dial Books, 1992), 117.

77 HWB 20. "Come and See." ©1974 Marilyn Houser Hamm. *Used with permission.*

78 HWB 388. Grant Us, Lord, the Grace.

79 "For God So Loved the World," by Frances Townsend. ©Singspiration Music, Zondervan Corp., Grand Rapids, Mich. 49506. From *Hymnal for Contemporary Christians* (Grand Rapids: Zondervan, 1974), 77.

81 SJ 13. My Soul Is Filled with Joy.

88 "God's Love Is for Everybody," song lyrics © 2001 Bryan Moyer Suderman. From the CD "God's Love is for Everybody: Songs of Faith for Small and Tall" by Bryan Moyer Suderman (Mennonite Church Canada/Faith and Life Resources, 2002), distributed by SmallTall Music (www.smalltallmusic.com) and Herald Press (www.heraldpress.com).

89 "How to work out conflict . . ." © Elkind+Sweet Communications/Live Wire Media. *Reprinted by permission.* Copied from www.GoodCharacter.com.

95 HWB 389. Take My Life and Let It Be.

96 From Craig Haas, *Mennonite Writings New and Old* (Intercourse, PA: Good Books), 311.

Scriptures

NOTE: The numbers indicated are the number of the devotionals, not the page numbers.

Index of Themes

NOTE: The numbers indicated are the number of the devotionals, not the page numbers.